A COMPREHENSIVE COURSE ON

CLIMBING

A COMPREHENSIVE COURSE ON

CLIMBING

CONTRIBUTING EDITOR: MICHAEL GRAY

This book is intended as an introduction to climbing and
mountaineering, not as an alternative to professional training.
Climbers should always seek expert guidance and advice before climbing.
Climbing carries a very real danger of death or serious personal injuries.
Anyone taking part in these activities should be aware of, and accept, these
risks, and be responsible for their own action and involvement.
The publisher and authors can accept no responsibility for any accident or
injury that may occur after reading this book.

Oceana

An Oceana Book

This book is published by
Oceana Books
The Old Brewery
6 Blundell Street
London N7 9BH

ISBN 1-86160-294-4

QUMTCL

Project Manager: Rebecca Kingsley
Project Editor: Maria Costantino
Editor: Sarah Harris
Designer: Bruce Low

Full picture credits listed on p.128

Typeset in Gill Sans
Manufactured in Singapore by
Pica Colour Separation Private Limited
Printed in Singapore by
Star Standard Industries (Pte) Ltd

Contents

Introduction

This book is intended to be a handbook for those seeking an introduction to rock climbing as a pastime. It should be noted that this book is intended only as an introduction to climbing and mountaineering. Whilst we believe everything in the book to be correct to the best of our knowledge, climbers should always seek professional training and advice from a recognised climbing centre before going climbing.

The aim of each section of the book is to allow the novice climber to progress as far as possible with the minimum of equipment. The first techniques discussed describe exercises which can be practised using only a pair of climbing boots and a chalk bag. Subsequent chapters look at climbing techniques and skills which require more equipment in order to master the different methods safely and effectively.

Sheer rock faces can make for an exhilarating climb.

COMMON ROUTES INTO CLIMBING

Climbing means different things to different people. To some it may mean scaling vast mountains, or navigating a rocky buttress in the rain and sleet. For others it means making athletic moves just a few feet from the ground; it may also conjure up pictures of climbing walls and fierce competition. There are also those whose climbing dreams involve clipping bolts on sun-kissed rock.

Climbers can be divided into two main groups: 'mountaineers' and 'rock athletes'. Mountaineers tend to have hill-walking backgrounds. From this starting point the hill-walker may wish to take on a bigger challenge by moving onto the rocky buttresses of the hillsides (or into the steep gullies). This type of easy climbing on hills is called 'scrambling'. It can be practised with a minimum of equipment, although a degree of skill is necessary in terms of general mountaineering ability, navigation, guide book interpretation, route-finding and judgement.

Rock athletes, on the other hand, may have started climbing on city walls, boulders or indoor climbing walls. They may very quickly rise up through the 'grades' of climb in terms of technical difficulty because the ability to make tricky athletic moves is their main aim. This group of climber may never need to navigate and could satisfy a lifetime's climbing urges without ever braving the elements.

Many people's idea of climbing focuses on huge peaks, such as these in Nepal's Langtang Valley.

satisfying approach to climbing. In this way you can best achieve the skills needed to make fluent athletic moves on rock, while still appreciating and enjoying the beauty of the mountain environment.

THE PSYCHOLOGY OF CLIMBING

Another important aspect of climbing is the risk factor. Risk and perceived risk are, for many climbers, at the very heart of their enjoyment. Facing fear, being able to overcome that fear and finishing the climb safely is one of the most satisfying and rewarding experiences any climber could hope for. In many ways climbing is a psychological game. For example, when the perceived risk of injury is high, a climber's main fear is falling. When in the grip of this fear, all movement becomes difficult; your mind races and you imagine every possible worst-case scenario. You grip the rock much harder than necessary, meaning that your arms soon become tired, and your fear of letting go and falling becomes even stronger. What are you to do? The solution is very simple, but at the same time extremely difficult – stay calm and relaxed.

When your head is calm and relaxed you can achieve your purpose much more easily. When gripped by fear even the simplest task seems impossible. Throwing yourself into situations which will test your cool is what climbing is all about. Being able to overcome the rising fear and making sensible decisions and free flowing movements on the rock face is a very satisfying experience indeed. It is also an ability which will serve you well in many other areas of your life.

That said, climbing does not have to be such an intense psychological experience. A lifetime's climbing could be done in 'safe' environments such as on boulders, climbing walls and bolted climbs. However, even in these contexts there is some degree of perceived risk and it is this which constantly draws people back for more.

Overcoming fear is one of the most satisfying experiences for a climber.
(Buachaille Etive Mor, Glencoe, Scotland)

Neither group of climber is less skilled nor less dedicated than the other. They both represent very valid approaches into the sport and indeed, in many ways, they are different means to different ends. The mountaineer rock climber might not be motivated by the hardest grade, preferring instead a long route in the mountains; the athletic rock climber may not relish the thought of a three-hour walk to the crag, instead preferring to make for a hard climb closer to the road.

The best that can be said is that the wider your experience and appreciation of the sport, the more you are likely to gain from it. Combining the different skills required by both the mountaineer and the rock athlete is probably the most

Mixed Climbing requires special protective
equipment and extra preparation.
(Buachaille, Glencoe)

Starting Out

VISUALISATION

As with so many other things, a little preparation can make a difference to your performance and enjoyment of climbing. There are many activities which could come under the banner of 'preparation' – warming up the body and stretching are only the most obvious ones. Visualisation is also one of the most important parts of preparation. Before leaving home it is useful to be able to imagine completing every stage of your proposed endeavour, from getting to the venue in the car to reaching the foot of the crag, from climbing each pitch of the route, to descending the hill safely. If you can't visualise yourself doing it, it's very unlikely you will succeed.

Visualisation of what you're about to do also allows your intuition to come into play. Although not everyone believes in intuition, it can be a useful tool. The great climber Reinhold Messner talks in his books of using his thoughts and dreams to guide his actions. His intuition in decision making is unparalleled and this at least partly explains his success in being the first man to climb all of the world's 8000 metre peaks.

Visualising your destination is exellent preparation when planning your route.
(Stupa-Namche Bazaar, Solo Kumba, Nepal)

Of course it is likely that while visualising your chosen route you may feel fearful about the task ahead. This is only natural. What you must be able to visualise is yourself overcoming those barriers and safely reaching your goal. If there is some underlying bad feeling about what you're about to try, or for some reason you can't visualise safely reaching the ground again, it is worth leaving well alone and choosing a different route.

Visualisation is also extremely useful during your climb. Upon reaching the hard moves (the 'crux') of the climb, it often pays to visualise yourself climbing it first. If you can see yourself doing it, you are almost there.

BREATHING TECHNIQUES

Along with visualisation, another simple technique can be extremely useful for calming a whirring, panicked brain. Slow, steady breathing into the lower abdomen has a marked effect on the way we think and feel. When we are relaxed, we breathe deeply and slowly into the lower abdomen using the diaphragm muscle. Similarly, consciously breathing deeply into the belly helps us to feel relaxed. Thoughts slow down or evaporate completely and the heart rate slows. This simple technique can be used to great effect both in preparation and during the course of a climb. Slowing the mind has a number of benefits for our climbing. Most obviously the brain uses less oxygen – leaving more for your muscles. Also the brain's mental capacity is then available to guide, steer and relax your muscles accurately rather than wasting energy on superfluous thoughts. Thirdly, the lower the level of fear and anxiety, the easier it will be for your brain to coax your body into making those few delicate moves.

WARMING UP

While climbing is one of the most natural and inbuilt faculties of the human being, it can carry the risk of injury, and not only from falling. Fingers were not really designed to support the entire human body, especially when grasping a tiny hand hold.

Warming up properly can greatly reduce the chances of injury to both muscles and ligaments. More than that, a good warm up will also increase the pleasure of climbing. How much time you need to spend warming up often depends on where you are climbing. Often the longer rock climbs or those in mountain situations can only be reached after a long walk with a heavy rucksack full of climbing ropes and equipment. By the time you've reached the foot of the crag you will be feeling very hot, making a warm up seem pointless. However, pausing to rest for a time will allow the body to cool off, at which point a warm up involving a few good exercises would be beneficial.

A warm up is most important in situations where the walk to the climb is minimal, and the climbing starts off with hard steep moves. The indoor climbing wall is the perfect example. You get out of the car, change and move straight onto some steep and thin moves on the bouldering wall. In these circumstances, straining injuries can easily occur.

Another common mistake is to assume that a few

Climbing is strenuous, and requires stamina and flexibility.
(White Heart, White Tower, Pembroke)

stretches constitute a warm up. Stretching is not warming up. Warming up should leave you feeling hot and sweating. Stretching cannot do this. Therefore warming-up must involve some kind of cardiovascular exercise like jogging, running on the spot, or anything which gets your heart pumping faster. Rowing, cycling or cross-country skiing machines are also excellent warming up exercises.

It is worth understanding a little about the process of warming up to see why it is so important to do it properly. When we take exercise, the working muscles are the first to warm up. The heart beats faster and our breathing rate increases to pass blood and oxygen around the body to our working muscles. The body's inner core starts to heat up too and we begin to feel

Warm-up exercises are essential to ensure your muscles and ligaments are supple enough to cope with the strain.

Suppleness and flexibility are more important for a successful climber than sheer strength.

warm. However, the extremities and the ligaments which will have to take the strain, such as the tendons in the wrists and hands, have barely begun to warm up. Therefore it is necessary to continue warming up until every part of the body is warm, not just until we feel warm.

SUPPLENESS OVER STRENGTH

It is an old climbing adage that women make better natural climbers than men. This is not necessarily because women have more natural climbing ability, but more a symptom of the way they approach things. Because women have less physical strength than men, they tend to find ways of doing things which require less strength. They may use more technique, incur less wasted effort, and save strength by being more relaxed. All of these apply in the context of climbing.

However, another two innate faculties of women help them climb with more apparent ease than men – suppleness and balance. Women tend to be more supple than men. In the climbing context this means that less upper body strength is required. Similarly, better balance means that less strength in the arms and hands is required. Why should women have better balance? Simply because they have a lower centre of gravity. More importantly though, because women generally have less upper body strength than men, or perhaps are just less inclined to show it off, they tend to rely more on suppleness and balance. This obviously improves these faculties, in turn making them even more useful.

Suppleness reduces the level of strength required and allows you to keep more weight on your feet. Suppleness, especially around your hips and sides means that your bodyweight can be taken on your feet for more of the time. A high step instead of a gruelling pull-up, or a wide bridge with your legs instead of arms alone can save huge amounts of strength and effort. We will return to the techniques of climbing in the next chapter.

Climbing Without Ropes

This chapter looks at the basic techniques needed to climb well. These techniques are covered under the following headings: *Good Footwork, Bouldering in the Outdoors, Climbing Walls, Games on Walls, and The Ladder Mentality.* All of the methods in this section can be mastered without the use of a rope. It is surprising just how good you can become at climbing without ever having touched a rope or needing a climbing partner. However, for obvious safety reasons, you will need to stay close to the ground when learning to climb without the use of a rope.

The beauty of learning this way is that the early development of your climbing ability, and therefore your enjoyment, is not reliant on mastering the complexities of roped protection. Many more moves can be practised when 'bouldering' close to the ground than can be made when using ropes and protection. It makes sense, therefore, to learn to become a good natural climber first, and learn about ropes and protection after having developed some basic skill on the rock.

Maintaining bodyweight largely through the feet is the mark of a good climber.

Bouldering is a good way to pratice moves without having to learn complicated rope manoeuvres.

Nothing beats the feeling of climbing on rock, but there are many important ground rules and techniques which should be learnt beforehand, and there are a few 'tricks of the trade' worth describing. These are moves or techniques that may not feel entirely natural at first, but are worth persevering with, as they can often take years to discover by chance.

GOOD FOOTWORK

The first concept to grasp is that standing on your feet is much easier than trying to support your body weight with your hands. This may seem obvious, but on the rock it is often far from easy to trust your feet on tiny sloping holds. It is often easier to place your weight on your feet only when you feel safe. The more tense you become, the more difficult it becomes to trust those little footholds. Consequently, your hands end up taking most of the strain. This in turn soon tires out those critical forearm muscles which only further heightens the level of fear or tension being experienced. The mark of a good climber then, is someone who is able to keep almost all of their weight on their feet in almost any situation.

Small moves are best when choosing a handhold.

A good way to 'start off on the right foot' is to visualise the way you are going to climb before actually putting foot to rock. Visualise your hands barely clasping the holds before you. Imagine yourself simply walking across the wall, only using your hands as a kind of support. As you then start to climb, you will do so much more efficiently. When you're not moving across your chosen boulder problem, try to find a position where your hands are taking a minimum of the strain. Try to let as much weight off your hands as possible. As you do so, you will feel more weight coming to bear on your feet.

As you think about making a move, the first thing you will naturally do is to look for a good handhold. To begin with, try to make small moves rather than long ones, which are more likely to cause soft tissue injury if you are not completely warmed up. Looking down to choose the best foothold is more difficult. Not only does your body obstruct your view, but lying out from the wall puts more strain on your fingers. It is essential, however, to make a good choice of foothold. Swinging up on your arms because your feet are resting on next to nothing, or are in the wrong position will tire your arms out in no time, no matter how strong you are. A common mistake in the beginning is placing one foot on a hold too far off to one side, probably because it looked like a good one. The result of this is to bring your feet out of line, when they should be directly below your bodyweight. Once again, this places more of the strain onto your hands.

Supple legs and hips are a great asset for a climber. They make it much easier to keep weight on your feet and off your hands. To understand this, try a little experiment on the bouldering wall.

Make a high step for a foothold in front of you. Imagine that your hips are a bit stiffer than they really are. As you move up on the high foothold you'll see that your body weight has to come some distance out from the wall in order to move up past the 'stiff' hip. Because your bodyweight has come away from the wall, your hands are taking more of the strain. Now try the same move after a warming up exercise. The suppleness in your hips keeps the pelvis (and the rest of your bodyweight) close to the climbing surface. This means that nearly all of the force necessary to move your bodyweight in an upwards direction can be delivered by the leg, and legs are so much stronger than arms.

Feet can be placed in a number of standard ways. One classic climbing stance is to stand sideways on the rock surface. This means that on one side the outside edge of your foot is placed on the holds while the other side uses the inside edge. This stance allows your bodyweight to stay close to the rock, and allows good visibility to the feet area to see those essential footholds.

Bouldering at sunset.
(Craigs of Kyle, Ayrshire, Scotland.)

BOULDERING IN THE OUTDOORS

In some ways bouldering embodies the true spirit of climbing. It is all about the freedom to move on rock unhindered by clutter. The term bouldering refers to climbing on boulders or small crags. Bouldering is generally practised without ropes or equipment, and you are generally climbing close enough to the ground to avoid injury should you fall or jump off. A good bouldering venue, close to your home, is one of the best assets you could possibly have as a novice climber. Moves can be practised over and over again without the loss of time involved in learning to use ropes and equipment. Very difficult manoeuvres can be perfected just a metre or so from the ground. Thus in an evening's bouldering you may be able to cover more rock than in a whole day's climbing on a hard route.

Rather than talk about a 'route' which is only a couple of metres long, climbers prefer to use the word 'problem'. A 'boulder problem' is a particular move or series of moves on a boulder. Because bouldering isn't always entirely safe, it is also very good for learning the ability to climb under pressure. One moment you may be confidently making hard moves above neatly clipped green grass; a few moves to one side and you suddenly find that moves above the jagged boulders are so much

During a good bouldering session, you can cover more rock than on a harder route. (Col de Montets, Chamonix Valley, France)

Bouldering allows you to enjoy climbing without clutter. (Fontainbleu, France)

harder to make. The psychological game inherent in climbing becomes apparent. It's not just being able to make the moves on the rock which is so satisfying, but being able to make them in a situation of perceived (or very real) risk. Climbers often talk about the 'landing' below a particular boulder problem. In a way this equates to the 'protection' available on a longer route. A good landing means that you can fall or jump without serious consequences.

In some situations it may be worth using a rope the first time you try a particular boulder problem. This may be because the hard moves are high off the ground, or because there is a particularly bad landing. Often, after practising the problem a few outweighs any negative reservations based on traditional values. Suffice to say that indoor walls now have their place in the overall 'climbing scene' as training aid and safe places to start learning. It is always worth remembering though that they represent only a tiny fraction of the overall pastime of climbing.

There are a few points worth bearing in mind about climbing on walls. Firstly, unless you cycle or jog to the local wall, there is no natural warm up before you start climbing. This, combined with the fact that indoor walls tend to be very steep (i.e. overhanging), means that the risk of soft tissue injury tends to be higher on indoor walls. In addition, because of the good landings and crash mats' on the floor you are more likely to try climbing on tiny holds and pull round outrageous overhangs. Therefore, a proper warm up and a good body stretch is never more essential than when at the climbing wall. Once your inner core is warmed up properly, remember to make sure that your extremities are also thoroughly warmed. Try a few 'helicopters', (swinging straight arms round and round from the shoulder joint) which forces warm blood out into the finger tips by means of centrifugal force. Then, with one hand, massage down the forearm and out along each finger of the other hand. Both the hand being massaged and the hand doing the massaging will be getting warmed up.

Bouldering allows the climber to practise difficult moves close to the ground.

times with a rope, it is possible to dispense with the rope and forever after be able to climb the problem without protection. Decisions such as when to use the rope, and when to dispense with it, can only be made by you on the basis of all your acquired experience and your intuition.

CLIMBING WALLS

More and more of us have our first climbing experience indoors, at a local climbing wall. In some respects this is a little sad, as so much of the fun derives from being outdoors the wilderness and the adventure. However, the benefits which indoor climbing walls have brought both to experienced climbers and to those entering the sport far

Bouldering at Joshua Tree National Monument, USA.

GAMES ON WALLS

There are three main ways to use a climbing wall. In the first instance, with no knowledge of ropes or belaying, it is usually possible to boulder on the wall. Most indoor walls have at least one dedicated bouldering wall complete with crash mats underneath. To use this kind of wall all you need do is put on your climbing boots, warm up properly and start climbing. Like bouldering outdoors, it is possible to get more climbing done, making more moves over the climbing surface, when not using the ropes.

The next step up is commonly called 'top roping' but is more correctly, if confusingly, called 'bottom roping'. The climber has a rope attached to the climbing harness which runs through a pulley at the top of the wall. Hence the term top roping, because the rope is always above the climber. The person holding the rope (the belayer) is standing on the ground, taking in rope as the climber moves up. Hence the term 'bottom roping' because the belayer is standing at the bottom of the climb. Therefore correctly speaking, top roping is when the rope is above the climber, and the belayer is above the climber at the top of the pitch. However, people do tend to use both terms synonymously. This will be covered in more detail in a later chapter.

The third game to play on the wall is 'leading'. Leading is where the climber 'leads' the rope out. There is no rope above the climber. Rather, the climber clips the rope through 'runners' which are already in place on the wall. Leading is psychologically and physically more demanding than bottom roping. Firstly, because there is no rope above you while climbing, a fall will necessitate travelling through the air for some distance before the fall is arrested. The distance fallen will be at least twice the length of rope between the climber's harness and the last runner clipped (assuming the climber's harness is above the clipped runner). The fact that a short fall will ensue should your climbing prowess let you down makes the moves seem that bit more difficult. Leading is more physically demanding because at each runner you will need to hang on with one hand while the other grabs the rope and clips it through the runner.

Many people will argue that it is worthwhile to get used to falling off when climbing on the relatively safe runners in the climbing wall. Some even recommend jumping off the wall from above your last runner to get used to the feel of it. The reasoning is that the more you trust the equipment to hold you, the less you will suffer from the psychological stress of

Many people's first experience of climbing is on an indoor wall.

worrying about falling off while you are climbing. Hence you will climb better. There is a lot of truth in this argument. However, do bear in mind that when you climb outside, on runners you have placed yourself, and on rock of unpredictable quality, there is no guarantee that your runners will stay in place. Then you will either be climbing confidently with false security, or you will now have to learn to climb while dealing with the fear of injury.

If you do choose to deliberately fall off at the wall, choose an overhanging wall where you will not hit anything on the way down, and make sure the person holding your rope is concentrating and doing their job properly.

THE LADDER MENTALITY

Before the invention of climbing walls it probably would not have been necessary to write about something known as 'the ladder mentality'. This refers to the idea that the hands are always in the position they would be in on a ladder, and the feet are always just stepping up from one obvious hold to another. Occasionally, indoor climbing walls can have too many routes which can be climbed in this way. If you stick to these routes, it will be difficult to move onto natural rock without something of a shock. Also there will be little fun in climbing if every move is roughly the same. Therefore try to pick routes which are not simply lines of bucket-sized jug handles all the way to the top. The enjoyment comes from trying to work out what to do to overcome a particular problem. This is sometimes called 'reading the rock' and is an essential skill for climbing in the wilds. Unfortunately, climbing walls do not really allow the beginner to develop this particular skill. If you're on orange holds, then the next hold is orange, it is obviously seen from where you are, and it is also usually fairly obvious which way you might be able to hold it in order to move up.

Not so in the outdoors (unless the route you are on is 'chalked up', i.e. the holds are covered in chalk from the last person who climbed it). All you are likely to be faced with then is a wall of rock. Trying to work out which bits to hold on to and how, and which to stand on and how, is much of the challenge and the fun. Therefore, in the early days of your climbing career try not to practise exclusively on indoor walls. Outdoor boulders and crags are the best learning aids, and in cities railway embankment walls and occasionally buildings are used for climbing practise.

Climbing walls provide a safe environment for mastering many of the basic techniques.

Summer Rock Climbing

INTRODUCTION

This section takes a look at summer rock climbing in 'cragging' situations. The term cragging usually refers to climbing near enough to the road or civilisation so that the paraphernalia associated with mountaineering maps and compasses, emergency survival gear etc is not required. Cragging, therefore does not usually require a long walk in, nor a great deal of planning. Usually some basic climbing equipment, and perhaps something to eat and drink will be enough.

However, do not expect that all crags are therefore safe and easy. You should always be aware of the possible descent routes from the top of the crag before leaving the ground. Some crags demand an abseil descent so you might be advised to carry some 'tat' – tape sling which will be left behind as an anchor for the abseil ('ab') rope. However, in some areas of the world environmental protocols may prevent the climber from leaving colourful tat hanging on the crag. So always check and follow the local guidelines.

Other crags may have steep grass descent routes at the side of the crag. Bear in mind just how slippy rock shoes are on grass and, if necessary, carry training shoes to walk down in. It is an old climbing dictum that "ninety percent of accidents happen in descent". While this may never have been proved statistically it is still worth bearing in mind. The jubilation and exhilaration of finishing a route often sweep away the awareness of danger, which was so acute while the climb was still in progress. However, sometimes the descent can be as, if not more, dangerous than the ascent.

Where to gear up or rest at the foot of the crag is also a decision that needs to be given careful thought. The temptation is to walk right to the bottom of the cliff and sit down at the foot of the routes. However, here you will be directly in the fall line of any loose stones or dropped climbing gear. For this reason choose a safe area to gear up and eat lunch free from the danger of falling objects. Only remove your helmet when away from the base of the crag.

Soloing is only for the very experienced. There is no room for nerves or mistakes.

Cragging is generally considered safe, but common sense and care are still essential.
(Steal Hut Crag, Scotland)

Unfortunately, in some areas, theft has become a problem at popular climbing venues. The unscrupulous soon learn that climbers often carry expensive equipment around in their rucksacks and their cars while at the same time being safely out of the way for a period of time. The best advice perhaps is not to bring anything you won't need in the first place. Park somewhere which is in good view from the crag or other public places. Unfortunately, avoiding the theft of your rucksack at the bottom of the crag is a difficult matter. Again, it is a good idea to leave it in full view of the crag if possible, but the best advice is simply to leave behind anything you don't really need and carry valuables in your pocket while on the crag.

Cragging also provides some wonderful sight-seeing opportunities.
(Pine Wall Crag, Poll Dubh, Glen Nevis)

Rock Climbing Equipment and its use

This section covers the main items of equipment used in rock climbing and give an explanation as to their use. In addition it is necessary to describe something of the physics of arresting a fall to ensure that the decisions you make while protecting a route are based on an understanding of the underlying principles.

Protection in climbing depends upon a whole set of elements known as the safety chain and, as everyone knows, a chain is only as strong as its weakest link. The safety chain includes the climber's harness, the knots, the rope, the karabiners which the rope is clipped through and their extenders, the runners placed in the rock (and the rock itself), the belay device, the belay anchors, the belayer and his harness. As you can see there are quite a number of links in the chain. Just one weak link and the entire chain will be rendered useless. Provided the climber has done everything correctly, the weakest link in the safety chain is usually the rock itself.

HARNESSES AND BUCKLES

Harnesses must be used in accordance with the manufacturers' instructions. The buckles on harnesses are notorious for their ability to be fastened incompletely or incorrectly. A useful rule is to stop all conversation when you are putting on your harness and fastening the buckle. If someone speaks to you,

Harness with buckle done up.

ignore them until the job is finished properly. The same rule applies to the tying of knots. This will prevent you from starting climbing on a half fastened buckle, or a half-tied knot.

Many harnesses are still made in such a way that the tape waist belt must be doubled back through the buckle. This means the harness can be worn with the buckle being incompletely fastened. Make sure you read the instructions, and do it properly every time.

Most makes of harness have a number of constituent parts. The waist belt is usually made of wide tape and is the main load-bearing part of the harness. Below this are the leg loops, which also take some of the body weight. At the front is usually a belay loop, which may be used to attach a belay or abseil device, or to clip yourself into a belay. In addition, most harnesses have gear loops at the sides and perhaps at the back. These loops are for 'racking' your protection only. A fatal flaw for beginners is to clip into one of the gear loops on a belay, or clip the belay device to one to protect a partner. This is lethal because the gear loops are usually only designed to hold a weight of about 15 kilograms. In contrast the belay loop is usually designed to hold a weight of 2000 kilograms.

This is one main reason why you should never have clothing hanging over the harness while you are climbing. Make sure that all clothing is tucked down inside the harness so that all buckles, loops and knots remain in full view. This way you will be less likely to do something stupid, such as clip into the wrong loop. Make sure that the waist belt is done up tightly enough so that the harness cannot be pulled down over the hip bones. Remember it is possible to flip upside down while hanging in a harness, and if this happens the last thing you will want to do is slip out of the harness.

ROPES AND KNOTS

Climbing ropes have come a long way since the early days of roped rock climbing. At one time ropes were made of hemp, which meant they did not stretch at all. Modern ropes on the other hand are made with elasticity in mind. It is the elasticity in the rope which will reduce the impact forces in the case of a fall. A little arithmetic here will help.

Newtons law states that:

Force = Mass x Acceleration (f=ma)

Arresting a fall obviously involves deceleration rather than acceleration, and so:

Force = Mass x Deceleration (f=md)

The rate of deceleration is given by the change in speed of the falling climber, divided by the length of timetaken for that change in speed:

(d=ΔS/t)

Therefore the greater the length of time taken to arrest a fall, the lower the rate of deceleration. In turn, the lower the rate of deceleration, the lower the forces generated in the system. Now imagine that you arrest a fall with a rope that does not stretch. The entire deceleration would need to take place within a split second or two. Because this time is so short, the impact forces generated on the safety chain would be huge. It is for this reason that climbing ropes are made elastic. The rope stretch in a fall lengthens the time over which the deceleration occurs and hence reduces the forces on the entire system. Clearly this means that the more rope there is between the falling climber and the belayer, the less the impact forces are likely to be. These impact forces are given by the 'fall factor'

which is worked out as follows:

Fall Factor = Length of Fall / Length of Rope Out

So if there is 10m (32 feet) of rope out and the leader has climbed up 10m (32 feet) and placed no runners atall, the length of fall would be 20 metres (65 feet) assuming it is not the first pitch. In this case 20/10 = 2,therefore the fall factor equals 2. This is the maximum fall factor because the length of the fall is twice the length of rope out. Now suppose the leader had placed a runner at 5 metres (16 feet) and climbed another 5 before falling. The fall length would be 10m (32 feet) as would the length of rope out. Thus the fall factor would be equal to 1. The impact forces are still fairly large. Consider the same length of fall, however this time near the top of he pitch. Say the leader has climbed for 40 metres (131 feet) and again fallen off 5 metres (16 feet) above his last runner. The length of fall is the same, as because of the extra rope out the fall factor is now only 10/40 = 0.25. The lesson in this is that falls close to the belay are likely to generate higher forces than falls near the top of a pitch. For this reason, you should place a runner as soon after leaving the belay as possible, and keep runners closer together if possible near the start of a pitch.

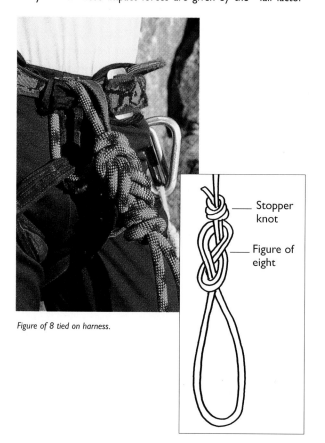

Figure of 8 tied on harness.

— Stopper knot

— Figure of eight

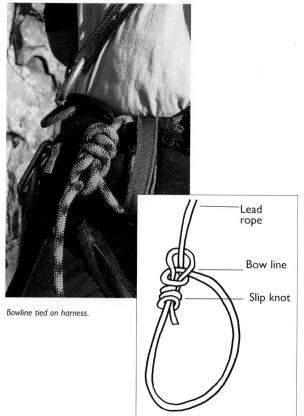

Bowline tied on harness.

— Lead rope

— Bow line

— Slip knot

GOOD BELAYING

A belay device must be able to pay out rope quickly and easily to the climber as upward progress is made, while at the same time being able to generate friction should the climber fall off. Some older types of belay device tend to grab the rope when paying out rope quickly. For this reason newer models have been designed with freer running belaying in mind. However, this does means that the newer devices are less forgiving should the belayer not be holding the rope correctly when a fall takes place.

Most devices have two slots for double rope climbing. A bight of rope is forced though the slot and clipped to a screw gate karabiner which is attached to either the belay loop on the climbing harness or to the loop of rope tied to the harness. Using the rope loop provides the advantage of having a little extra stretch to absorb the impact forces in the event of a fall. The karabiner used for belaying should be of HMS variety and should have a round cross section. This means that the rope is not turning tight corners as it runs through the plate and round the krab. It also means that there is a greater mass of metal to dissipate the heat generated when the device is used under load.

The photographs demonstrate good belaying technique. The rope between the belay device and the climber is called the 'live' rope. The rope on the other side of the device from the climber is called the 'dead' rope. It is imperative that there is always a hand firmly holding the dead rope. It is the dead rope which can control the action of the belay device in generating friction.

Belaying is described using the right hand as the control hand (i.e. on the dead rope) for ease of description. You must however be able to belay on both sides and the reasons for this will become apparent in the section on making belays. To take rope in through the plate, start with the left hand at arm's length from the belay device up the live rope. The right hand holds the dead rope close to the belay device. The dead rope is pushed upward parallel to the live rope, which is pulled in. The rope will run smoothly through any belay device provided that the push and pull are carried out simultaneously so that no slack rope forms on the live side, which can jam the device. As the left hand

Belaying, taking rope in. Push-pull to bring in rope keeping both ropes straight to prevent the plate from catching.

Lock-off the plate at and bring the other hand across to hold the dead rope. This allows the control hand to be moved up again close to the plate.

Keeping the plate locked off – waiting to take in again.

comes close to the belay device and the right is outstretched the device must be 'locked off'. This means that no rope can pass through the device as the positions of the hands are readjusted. To lock off the device, the right hand is brought down by the hip so that the dead rope is at an angle of 180° to the live rope (i.e. in a straight line through the plate). To readjust the position of the hands it is imperative never to let go of the dead rope. Therefore the left hand is brought across to hold the dead rope so that the right hand can be moved back to hold the dead rope again close to the belay device. The left hand is then once again placed high on the live rope ready to take in again.

NEVER let go of the dead rope while belaying, and never attempt to save time or effort by simply sliding the right hand up the dead rope. ALWAYS bring the left hand over to hold the dead rope in order to move the right hand up to the device again.

The above sequence can be summarised very simply 'push-pull, lock-off, left-right'.

While belaying you should be able to see your climbing partner at all times and should watch him or her closely. Be prepared to give out rope quickly when the leader is about to clip a high runner. If belaying a second climber from above or on a bottom rope system, neither keep the rope too tight (unless asked to do so) nor too slack. The rope should be straight, but not tight.

FALLING OFF

Should the leader fall off unexpectedly while belaying in this way, there will always be a hand on the dead rope to arrest the fall. If the rope through the device is not at an angle of 180° then rope will run through the device. Therefore the belayer's reaction should be to lock off the plate as soon as the fall is perceived. This is done simply by bringing the control hand (i.e. the hand holding the dead rope) down to the hip so that the rope through the device forms an angle of 180°. A small amount of rope slippage may occur though the device although this should not endanger the climber. Indeed, because rope slippage decreases the rate of deceleration for the falling climber, it will also reduce the shock load forces on the runners and/or the anchors.

THE NECESSARY HARDWARE

A typical rock climbing rack you would be likely to carry for a route on the crag would include helmet, harness (with pen-knife and prusik loops attached), rock boots, rope, sling and screw gate

Rock climbing equipment for a typical days cragging.

karabiner, guide book, at least one set of nuts (with sizes 1-5 on one krab and sizes 6-10 on another), a set of RP's, a selection of camming devices, a couple of hexes and a number of extenders. The exact selection of gear you choose for any particular route will be a judgement you must make from the ground. Are there likely to be very large cracks justifying carrying that size ten hex? Does the route really require RP's for micro cracks?

Sometimes local knowledge is very useful to help you decide what gear to take on a route. Occasionally one particular piece of gear is almost essential for a particular route. Knowing this in advance can make a huge difference to your chances of success.

PLACING ROCKS

Rocks are perhaps the most common form of protection used in rock climbing. A well-placed rock runner also provides one of the quickest, most efficient and secure anchors available. Rocks are most effective in places where cracks in the rock narrow to form constrictions. You need to develop an eye for the correct size of rock and this takes time and practice to get right first time. To place a rock runner, unclip the krab with your rocks on it from

the gear loop and sort out the right size of rock while still on the krab. Place the rock in the crack and give a steady downward pull to seat the rock in place. The temptation to 'chuck' should be avoided as this can make the rock difficult to remove. Once firmly seated, remove the krab with the remaining nuts on it and clip this back to your gear loop. Clip an extender to the placed nut, and clip the rope through the lower krab on the extender making sure that you clip it correctly.

As with all runners and anchors you must always be aware of the expected angle of force on the gear should it be loaded by a fall. This angle will be determined not only by the position on the falling climber, but also by the angle of the rope running back to the belayer. If, for example, you start climbing with a long horizontal traverse, place a runner, and then climb upwards. This way, if you fall, the angle of force on the runner will not be straight downwards but at 45° to vertical. This is because of the sideways pull generated by the rope running back from runner to belayer.

While it is obviously easier to use rocks in vertical cracks, they can also often be used to good effect in horizontal ones. However, a constriction is perhaps even more necessary to make the placement a good one. Occasionally upward-pull anchors are required in situations where the belayer is light in comparison with the leading climber. In this case gear can be placed upside down and the belayer tied down to it with a clove hitch on the rope or with a sling.

PLACING HEXES
Hexes are for use in wider cracks and can be used to good effect in more parallel-sided cracks than nuts. This is because they work on a different principle to rocks, which depend upon constrictions or irregularities in the rock. Used in its normal orientation a hex is designed to twist into a parallel-sided crack as it comes under load. Used sideways in a wider crack, the hex loses its twisting (or camming) action and so if a hex is used in this way it should be used at a constriction or narrowing of the crack.

PLACING CAMS
Like hexes, camming devices can be used in parallel-sided cracks in the absence of constrictions. They can be much faster to place than hexes although they can sometimes be difficult to place properly. Most importantly, the cams should be in the middle of their range. If the cams are only just touching the sides of the crack, the placement may be completely ineffective. Friends are also more likely to move around in the crack as the

Well placed offset rock

Well placed rock

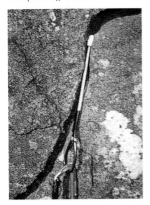

Well placed rock

Badly placed rock

A well placed hex in a parallel sided crack. Note how with the rope coming from the upper side the twisting action of the hex into the sides of the crack is better than with the rope coming from the lower side.

A hex in a vertical parallel sided crack.

A Size 3 HB Flexi-Fix in a horizontal crack. A camming device without a flexible stem would not be suitable in this situation unless tied off near the head with a tape sling.

rope is pulled through the runner. This is called walking in because as the friend is moved from side to side it tends to walk deeper and deeper into the crack. This is likely either to render the placement useless, or cause the friend to bottom out at the

A well placed camming device, in this case an HB Quadcam, in the mid-range of its camming action.

back of the crack. If the latter occurs it can be very difficult to remove the device. For these reasons friends should always, if possible, be extended to reduce the likelihood of them walking.

You should also be aware of the pitfalls of using camming devices in horizontal cracks. In particular the rigid stems on camming devices should not lie across the edge of the crack. This not only creates the risk that the stem will simply break, but also prevents the camming action from working properly. Instead of the straight pull required to produce the cam, the device is instead levered onto the top side of the crack. For this reason you should either use a flexible stemmed device in horizontal cracks, or tie off the rigid stem with a prusik loop near the cam and clip the rope into this instead. This will prevent the levering action on the head of the cam and the risk of breakage of the stem.

USING SLINGS

Tape slings can sometimes be used to good effect as runners. For example, anywhere a choke has formed in the rock, such as where a rock is jammed in a crack, can make for a good 'thread' runner using a sling. Simply thread the sling around the back of

Note how the gates face outwards so that the ropes run across the back bar of the each krab.

choked stone and clip the two ends together. Slings can also be used on rock spikes as runners. The danger with using a sling runner on a spike is that the whole sling can simply lift off the spike as the rope is pulled though the runner. Therefore it may be a good idea to weight the sling down with a couple of extenders or heavy krabs.

USING EXTENDERS TO MINIMISE ROPE DRAG

You will probably use one extender for each piece of protection placed, and so the number of extenders you carry may represent the maximum number of runners you get in any one pitch. Extenders can however be split so that you get two runners for each extender.

In the beginning it is advisable to climb on one 11mm (¹/2 inch) rope before graduating to two 9mm (¹/3 inch) ropes. Two ropes have a number of advantages, one of the most important being that they help to minimise rope drag. Rope drag occurs when the rope runs round too many corners. If, for example, your runner placements are not in a straight line, the rope will be forced to snake from side to side though each runner. Before long, pulling the rope through the zig-zag will generate so much friction that upward progress becomes difficult if not impossible. Using two ropes reduces rope drag by reducing the zig-zagging of the single rope. The runners on the left can be clipped by one rope, while the other rope can be clipped through the runners on the right.

Using extenders also significantly reduces rope drag. If you are using a single rope in the beginning, it is advisable to use long extenders so that the potential for rope drag can be minimised. When you graduate to the two-rope technique, these long extenders can gradually be replaced with shorter ones.

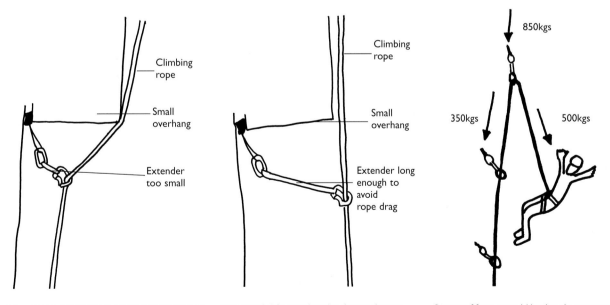

Rope not extended far enough causing increasingly severe rope drag.

Rope extended far enough so that the rope does not require to turn any sharp corners. As a result there is much less friction on the rope.

Diagram of forces exerted. Note how the top runner takes the maximum force. This is the most likely point of failure.

CLIPPING THE GEAR CORRECTLY

The top krab on an extender should always be positioned with the gate down and out from the rock. The easiest way to do this is to clip the krab through the gear with the gate open at the top and in towards the rock. Once clipped, the krab can then be turned through 180° so that it sits correctly. The bottom krab, through which the rope will run, must also be positioned correctly. Again the gate opening should be at the bottom and the gate away from the rock. In addition the rope to the climber should be running across the back bar of the krab. If the rope is running upwards across the gate of the krab the rope can actually unclip itself from the krab in the event of a fall. This is especially likely if the krab is of the easy clip variety.

MAKING BELAYS

Belaying involves the technique of safeguarding the climber using the rope. The belay is the stance from where the belaying is carried out. The belay therefore can be on the ground at the foot of the route, on the crag in between each pitch, or on the top of the crag. Belays may use trees, rock spikes or threads, or, most commonly, gear placed in the rock. You should always try to get at least two independent anchors, which combine to form the belay. This section is mainly concerned with how these independent anchors should be linked for safely.

The first choice you have to make is whether to use slings or rope to join the anchors back to the harness. The benefits of using rope are that it is fast to construct, and because of the dynamic qualities of the rope, the belay also has some shock-absorbing properties, which help to reduce the impact forces in a fall. Using the rope is best in situations where you and your climbing partner are leading through' i.e. you are eachalternately leading and seconding pitches. If, however, one climber is doing all the leading, using the rope to tie into belay stances is more awkward than using a sling. This is because you will have to switch position on the belay stance with the second climber, so a sling tied off to a central anchor point is easier to work with.

There is a simple set of three principles to follow when making any belay. They are summarised in the acronym VIE (which is French for "life"). This stands for Vector, Independent, and Equalised.

The vector part refers to the necessity of keeping the angle of the belay ropes at the central anchor point below 120° and preferably much lower. If the angle of the ropes running out to the anchors from the central point is

Using a single rope in a two point belay. The climbers rope is clove-hitched into the first anchor, then clove-hitched into the second anchor. Thirdly the rope is clove-hitched back to the climbers rope loop onto a screw gate krab. The hitches are adjusted so that the two load ropes are equally weighted.

greater than 120°, a downward force on the central point will generate a greater force on each of the anchors.

The anchors should be independent in the sense that if one anchor gives way, the central point does not move. This means that each side of the belay should be tied-off independently.

Thirdly, the loading on the anchors should be equalised so that the forces are shared between them. This is obviously preferable to having a slack rope in the belay with all the strain being taken on one anchor.

USING THE ROPE

With the double rope technique, making a two-point belay with the ropes could not be easier, especially if your anchor points are within reach of your desired belaying position. Simply place two good anchors in the rock, making sure that they will take the

Using two half ropes in a two point belay. Simply clove-hitch each rope into an anchor and adjust so that they are equally loaded. This belay is fast to make, is easily adjusted and has shock absorbing properties.

angle of pull which would result from a fall. Then clip a screw gate krab into each and clove hitch one rope into each anchor. The clove hitch should be clipped the right way around so that the load rope is closest to the back bar of the krab. Clove hitches have the advantage of being very easy to adjust and lock-off. Simply stand in position, pull the load rope up tight using the centre loop of the clove hitch knot, and then, placing a finger on top of the knot to hold the ropes in position, pull the dead rope up to tighten the knot around the krab.

If an anchor is out of reach, simply clip the rope though the distant krab and return to your desired belay position. Clip an HMS screw gate krab through the rope loop on your harness and clove hitch the rope into this krab. The clove hitch can then be adjusted as before to equalise the independent anchors. If both anchors are out of reach they can both be tied back into the same HMS screw gate krab in this way, however, you must not

use two clove hitches on one krab which is not of the HMS variety.

If using one rope to make a multiple point anchor, simply clove hitch into the first anchor if it is within reach of your chosen stance. Then run the rope across to your second anchor and clove-hitch it onto that. Bring the rope back down to the harness and clove hitch the rope again to a screw gate krab clipped to the rope loop on your harness. You will have made a triangle of rope using three clove hitches in which the two load ropes should be equally tight and the rope running between the anchors should be loose.

An alternative fast single rope belay can be made using a figure of eight knot around the rope loop on the harness. Clip the furthest anchor from your stance and bring the rope back down to the harness. Tie a figure of eight on the bight around the rope loop and make the remaining loop of rope created by tying the knot just long enough to clip into the remaining anchor. It is a little more difficult to load the anchors equally using this method, but with practise it is very fast and effective. It is especially useful when one anchor is far away and the other is very close. Many other methods exist for tying into multiple anchors, however these are generally variations on these techniques. All methods should incorporate the VIE principle. It is extremely useful to practise making multiple point belays in the comfort of your own home. This way when you arrive at the top of a pitch you will have a system in place to enact, without having to think too hard.

USING SLINGS

The simplest and most effective method of making a two-point belay using a sling is with a simple overhand knot. Clip the sling into one anchor and ascertain where the central point will lie by bringing the sling up to the second anchor. Tie an overhand knot where you think the central point should lie and clip the sling into the second anchor. Adjust the position of the overhand knot so that the weight is equally distributed on each anchor. Then simply clip your HMS screw gate krab through the two loops formed by the overhand knot. This belay is then made up of two equalised and independent anchors while only using one overhand knot. To adjust the length of slings in making belays simply use an overhand knot, which is quick and effective.

WHICH SIDE?

The need for careful thought does not end once you have tied into your multiple point belay successfully. You must also get your

A two point anchor belay using one sling with overhand knot in the middle. Note how the screw gate krab is clipped though the overhand knot so that one sling effectively forms two equally loaded locked off slings. This belay is useful if you and your partner are not leading through. It suffers from a lack of elasticity however.

belay position correct and correctly choose the side you use as the control hand in belaying in the rope. The principles are simple enough. You should not be pulled significantly to either side or into the rock in the event that your climbing partner falls off. In addition you must always be able to get the angle on the ropes though the belay device to a full 180° in order to lock-off the device. A fall often results in a twist on the belayer. For example, the belayer may be standing facing out, with the anchor ropes coming into the harness on the right hand side. A strong pull will therefore cause the belayer to twist to the right as the live climbing rope and the anchor ropes tighten into a straight line. If the belayer had been using the left hand as the control hand on the dead rope in this situation, the twist to the right would make it impossible to lock-off the plate. Therefore the belayer must always make sure that the control hand is on the same side as the anchor ropes. With the dead rope in the right hand, in the above example, a twist to the right will

not prevent the belayer from locking-off the belay device at 180°.

The ropes should also run through the device in a straight line. This means that when bringing up a second climber, the dead rope should be at the top of the device and the live rope at the bottom of the device. If not, there will be a twist in the system. When the second climber reaches the stance and is ready to lead-off on the next pitch, it will be necessary to change the orientation of the belay device so that the live rope now runs out of the top of the device and the dead rope enters it from beneath. You should naturally make sure your partner is securely tied in with a clove hitch before unclipping and turning round the device.

TYING OFF THE BELAY DEVICE

Tying off the belay device is useful to protect your partner and leaves both your hands free while racking the gear on a belay. To do this, a loop of the dead rope is passed though the belay krab to form a bight around the back bar. This bight is then half hitched a couple of times around the back bar.

STANCE MANAGEMENT

While belaying you should not allow the dead rope simply to dangle down the crag. Sooner or later it will become inexorably snagged and you will find yourself in a difficult situation. For this reason the rope(s) should be kept on the stance, either by piling onto a ledge (if there is one) or by butterfly coiling over the anchor ropes on the belay in the absence of a ledge. If your partner is not leading though on the next pitch, remember that your end of the rope will be on the bottom of the pile. Therefore you should re-pile the rope starting at the second's end and finishing with the leader's end back on top of the pile. If you do not take the time to do this, you are likely to give your belayer problems as he/she tries to feed out rope from the bottom of the pile.

GUIDE BOOKS

Guide books have developed for climbers to record and describe the routes which have been done on a crag or in a particular area. Interpretation of the climbing guide book is almost a skill in its own right. Take as much information as you can from any diagrams in the guide, which provide a pictorial description of the crag and its routes. If there is one obvious line on the crag, which can be identified as a route in the guide book, it is often possible to work out where the other routes go from their position relative to the obvious line. Look out for obvious features such as chimneys or large boulders at the foot of the crag.

To follow a guide book description you will need to understand some of the phraseology surrounding rock features. Here are a few you will encounter:

Arete: a very steep ridge up the crag

Chimney: a wide crack into which you can fit your whole body

Chockstone: a stone or boulder choked in a crack or chimney

Choss: loose dangerous rock

Corner: an inward corner in the rock face at roughly 90°

Crack: a crack can be any width up to the point where it becomes a chimney

Diédre: an open corner

Flake: a protruding blade or rock

Groove: a shallow or narrow corner

Gully: a large break in the crag wide enough to walk up

Open Book: a wide angled corner

Overhang: a section of rock steeper than vertical

Overlap: where an upper slab lies on top of a lower slab an overlap is formed

Slab: a fairly low angled area of smooth rock

Roof: an extreme overhang where rock forms a roof

Wall: a steep face of 60° to 90°

CLIMBING CALLS

Climbers have developed over the years a fairly universal system of climbing calls so that when climbing partners are out of sight of each other, each knows what the other is doing. These climbing calls are likely to differ from country to country but the following will give the general idea.

CLIMBING – The climber has left the ground or the belay and started to climb. The belayer therefore must be concentrating.

SAFE – The climber has reached a belay stance and is clipped into his anchors. The belayer can therefore remove the rope from the belay device.

TAKING IN – The climber on the belay above is taking in the slack rope arm over arm. Therefore the second climber should not be climbing after this call.

THAT'S ME – The second informs the climber above that all the slack has been taken in and the rope is now tight against the second's harness. The climber on the belay above now knows to clip the rope through the belay device.

CLIMB WHEN READY – The climber on the top belay informs the second that he has clipped him onto the belay device and is ready to start belaying him in.

CLIMBING – The second signals that he has started climbing. The climber on the top belay should now be able to start taking in rope through the belay device.

TIGHT – The climber wants the rope to be taken in tight.

SLACK – The climber wants more slack on the rope.

TAKE IN – The belayer should take in more rope though the plate perhaps because a loop of slack rope has formed as the second climbs up.

TAKE ME – The climber signals that he/she is about to fall off and asks for the belayer to be prepared to catch the fall by locking off the belay device.

The term 'wall' is used to describe a steep face of 60° to 90° (Finger in the Dyke, Bla Bhein, Isle of Skye)

Always choose your climb according to your ability – some are harder than others!
(Armadillo, Isle of Arran)

Summer Grades

Over the years, distinctly different open-ended grading systems for rock have developed throughout the world. Each system emphasises different aspects and all have their advantages and disadvantages.

In the USA, a single system (5.4 to 5.14 sub-divided a, b, c) is used for traditional and sport climbs. This means a 10m highly technical, bolt-protected sport climb will probably get a higher grade than a less technical 300m climb which is poorly protected and very serious. Which route is really the harder? For mountain or multi-day rock climbs in the States a Roman numeral (III, IV, IV etc) is added to denote length, seriousness etc.

In the UK and Europe the French numeric system (6a, b, c, 7a etc) is used generally to denote sports climbs protected by bolts. In the UK this is usually prefixed F6a etc to differentiate a sport climb from a traditional UK 6a.

In the UK, traditional rock climbs use an adjectival system of Difficult, Very Severe, E (Extremely Severe) 1, 2, etc. This works similar to the French adjectival Alpine grades (below) and takes into account length, seriousness, technicality, protection etc. To this is added a numerical grade with a, b, c, sub-divisions which defines the hardest move or moves (Very Severe 5a, E7 6b etc).

French adjectival Alpine grades (Assez Difficile - AD, Difficile - D, Très Difficile - TD etc) are widely used in mountain areas, especially in Europe and reflect length, seriousness, technicality, altitude etc. Throughout Europe (except the UK) Union of International Alpine Associations (UIAA) Roman numeral grades (III, IV etc with plus or minus) are added for traditionally protected rock (Très Difficile, V+ etc).

Australia and New Zealand also use an Arabic numerical system which starts at 12 and currently extends into the 30s while artificial climbs worldwide are graded A1, A2 etc , usually with plus or minus.

Trying to compare grading systems can be a nightmare. Best to test the water on something which looks and sounds well within your ability, and raise your grade from there. Do this by using the guidebook, looking and asking around to find a popular, easy classic which you are sure is within your ability.

Climbing Techniques

By their very nature, climbing techniques are not the easiest or most practical things to learn from a book, and this is one of the reasons you should always enrol on a course or consult an expert before beginning to climb – this book is intended as an introduction to climbing, not as a replacement for professional tuition. So many aspects of climbing stem from a natural ability built into the human species that the written word can never come close to describing it. There is really little substitute for hours spent on the boulders, walls and crags, although as in the chapter on climbing without ropes, there are several handy tips that can make your learning process much simpler. The techniques discussed are: the side pull; stepping through; switching feet; lay backing; back and footing; bridging; hand jams; finger jams; foot jams; crimps; smears and off-widths. These, it is hoped, are the primary methods used in everyday rock climbing.

THE SIDE PULL

Learning to use the side pull technique is often the best way to leave behind the ladder mentality. Using side pull holds also makes it necessary for you to place nearly all your bodyweight on your feet. The side pull technique utilises holds which are facing sideways, making it impossible to pull down on the hold. Instead the hold can only be used to pull sideways. However, this sideways pull is enough to keep your body in close to steep rock, thus keeping your weight on your feet. While you can't pull up directly on a side pull, you can use it to move up. In an antagonistic action, your foot pushes hard down on its hold while your hand pulls sideways on its hold. This will lift your body upwards to bring the next hand and foot holds within reach.

Often it is best if possible to keep your arm straight when side pulling (also called lay waying). As in many other climbing situations it is much more efficient to keep your arm straight and use the larger muscles in your shoulders and back to move.

STEPPING THROUGH

In many situations a good climbing stance is to side on to the rock. This keeps your body close to the rock, so putting more weight on your feet, and allows good visibility of the rock for footholds. The sideways stance is also very good for traversing, i.e. moving sideways across a wall or boulder. Traversing is something you will probably do quite frequently. It allows you to climb a long distance without getting too far off the ground. If you wish to traverse to the right, support your weight on your left leg. Then simply bring your right leg through between your left leg and the rock. You will then need to place your right foot on a hold using the outside edge of your boot. This position may now feel a little off-balance. Readjust your hand position and bring

Friction layway up the edge of a slab. Note how the heels are turned out to keep the bodyweight in towards the rock. This helps to prevent the dreaded barn door.

your left leg forward round the outside again. In this way you can begin walking across the rock face (given a good set of holds). It has to be said that this move is seen and used a lot more often on indoor climbing walls than in the outdoors. Maybe this is because people generally try more flamboyant moves in the relative safety of the indoor wall. However, sometimes it is useful on real rock in the outdoors.

SWITCHING FEET

Another move frequently associated with traversing is known as switching feet. When there are insufficient holds upon which to place your feet, it is often necessary to switch feet on a hold. Watch the way that experienced climbers do this. With the inside edge of one boot on the only foothold, flick your heel out to the side and quickly replace your other foot on the hold as it becomes available. Done correctly, it is almost possible to do it without taking your weight off your feet and legs at all.

LAY BACKING

Lay backing is used for climbing a steep corner crack or the edge of an arete. The muscles of your body are strongly antagonistic in the layback position. Your arms are pulling while your feet are pushing in the opposite direction. Therefore lay backing is a technique involving a 'pumping' motion, and it doesn't take long for your arms to tire out. Also it is a difficult position in which to place protection. A common fault while lay backing is to end up with your feet too close to your hands. In this position there is an enormous strain on your hands as the full force of your legs are pushing against them. Try then to keep your feet as low as possible when lay backing. How low you will be able to keep your legs depends on how much you feel you can trust your feet on the rock. If it is greasy and slippery you will need them high, if it is dry with good friction you may be able to keep them low. If they get too low, you are likely to slip off.

Try not to stay too long in the layback position. Stopping to think for a while is not going to make life any easier as your fingers will gradually run out of gripping power. Try to see where you are going to get into a rest position, either on a foothold, or in a bridging position, before embarking on a long section of lay backing. Again try to keep your arms straight at all times as this will reduce the strain on your muscles.

The other essential thing you will discover when lay backing in something called the 'barn door'. This is more prone to happen when lay backing an arete as opposed to a corner line. Simply, as you move up in the lay back

position, your body starts to swing out from the rock, like a barn door opening. In some situations it takes very good balance and technique to prevent the barn door scenario. One technique is to turn your head in towards the wall. This helps keep your weight closer to the climbing surface. Secondly, try turning your feet so that your heels are out from the wall and your toes are smeared on the holds. This tends to make your torso face the wall rather than sideways, helping to keep your body weight closer to the wall.

BACK AND FOOTING

A chimney is a large crack or fault in the rock wide enough to get your whole body inside. The back and foot technique is extremely useful for climbing chimneys. Unlike lay backing, back and footing isn't particularly 'pumpy'. It is much easier to pause

Looking down the Unicorn corner on Stob Coire nan Lochan, Glencoe, Scotland.

while back and footing, in order to look for good placements for protection. This is because most of the strain is taken by your legs while back and footing.

Back and footing is an ideal technique for climbing chimneys.
(Savage Slit, Coire an Lochain, Cairngorms)

To move upwards, place your arms across the chimney with the palms of your hands on the opposite surface, fingers pointing down. This allows your weight to be briefly taken by your arms while your legs are moved up as high as possible. Place one foot on the opposing wall, and the other on the wall your back is against. Get this foot as high as possible, underneath the seat of your pants. By pushing in opposing directions with your two feet, you should now be able to generate enough grip on the rock to move upwards using your legs.

BRIDGING

Bridging is an extremely useful technique in the art of gaining a rest. It is usually a technique used in corners or wide chimneys, although bridging can be used anywhere with enough angle in the rock surface to push on in opposite directions. Again, bridging uses antagonistic forces to generate enough friction to keep your hands and feet on the rock. Thus bridging can often be used when there are few or no footholds whatsoever. Whether bridging is possible depends on the nature and angle of the rock. Open book corners are obviously more difficult to bridge up than chimneys, and you will generally feel much safer on rough dry rock than on very smooth or greasy rock. Small side pull handholds can often be used while bridging corner lines, pulling away from the corner in a brief lay back position in order to move your feet higher. If no holds are present for your hands then your arms must bridge out too, with your palms against the rock and your fingers pointing outwards, or even slightly downwards.

As mentioned earlier, bridging is an essential skill in gaining a rest in many situations. One of the first things worth practising is to climb up a corner or wide chimney and then find a good bridge position across the corner. Take both hands off the rock and use your balance to take all of your weight on your feet. In this way you will quickly discover that it is often possible to get a good rest for both arms at once. Anywhere there is sufficient angle in the rock surface to position your centre of gravity directly above the footholds is a potential position for resting your arms.

Obviously bridging is another ability which is greatly enhanced by supple hips and legs. The more supple your hips, the wider you will be able to bridge and the more control you are likely to have over your feet in fully extended positions.

HAND JAMS

Some people love hand jamming while others detest it. There are a couple of different hand jamming techniques worth describing, and which one to choose at which time depends on both the size of crack you're climbing, and the size of your hand. The hand jam which feels most secure is probably the fist jam where the whole hand is used sideways in a crack. When the fingers of your hand are extended, the width of your palm of the hand can be narrowed by curling your hand inwards at the sides. When your fist is clenched your hand becomes significantly wider. This difference in width is used to make fist jams in cracks which are narrower than a fist, but wider than the curled palm. Slot your hand into a crack just wide enough to allow it in horizontally. As you clench your fist inside the crack, your fist will widen and press against the sides of the crack. With enough skill you will be able to move up using your jammed hand as a hold.

Other hand jams are used in cracks which are too narrow for a full fist jam. There are a number of variants of these hand jams which are described below. With the straight finger hand jam, rather than the sides of the hands being used, the fingers, heel and back of the hand are used to press out on either side of the crack. Insert your hand sideways into the crack with your thumb upwards (or outwards), then fold your hand closed with the fingers straight. This will cause the fingers and back of your hand to jam in the crack, hopefully sufficiently well to allow you to move up on it. In some situations it increases the security of the hand jam if your thumb is folded across the palm of your hand. This thickens the fleshy heel of the hand and so broadens the hand jam slightly. Another variant to try is hooking your thumb over your index finger. This further increases the width of the hand jam giving greater security in cracks which are too wide for the straight fingered hand jam.

One reason that some people are averse to jamming is because they find it painful. This may because of the bone structure in the hand, or it may just be because the skin of their hands still requires thickening. Another reason some don't like hand jams is because of the consequences when they fail suddenly. On rough rock, a fist jam which slips out unexpectedly is likely to leave rather a lot of skin behind. However, with practise you will begin to realise that a well placed jam does not come out so easily and confidence will grow.

FINGER JAMS

In cracks which are too small to get the knuckles into, finger jams can be used. A good finger jam can feel really secure once you get the feel for it. The most secure finger jam is with the thumb down. Place as much of your fingers as possible into the crack and, when in place, torque the wrist downwards to twist the

Top: Fist Jam. Above: Straight finger hand jam. The thumb is held across the palm to support the jam.

fingers securely in the crack. It is the torque provided by your wrist which gives the finger jam so much more security and effectiveness. Be careful to keep your wrist low as you move up past the finger jam.

Finger jams must also sometimes be done with the little finger down (with the thumb upwards and outwards). This is usually necessary where a long reach is required above the head, or where the crack is just too small for the index finger. This type of jam usually feels very insecure as only your smallest fingers are in the crack, and it is difficult to get any torque on your fingers to increase the grip.

FOOT JAMS

Foot jams are used in vertical cracks. They are only necessary when no other footholds can be seen to either side. If the crack is large enough to insert the foot in sideways a good foot jam will be possible. Twist your foot so that the outside edge of your boot

is downwards, i.e. the sole of your foot is facing inwards. Insert your foot into the crack and then twist it so that the inside edge of your boot is forced downwards in the crack. This will jam your foot firmly in the crack and should easily take your weight. Unlike other footholds, foot jams are not always easily removed again. A very well-placed foot jam can almost become stuck in a crack. The best way to get it out is to keep your nerve and twist the sole of your foot inwards again while pulling outwards on your foot. Like hand jams, the consequences of falling off the rock with a foot jam firmly in place are not pleasant, as this can lead to a broken ankle. Therefore be careful to take good handholds while you are practising the foot jamming technique.

Finger jam making use of constriction in the crack.

Note the finger jam of the upper hand. The downward twist exerted from the elbow helps to keep the fingers in place in the vertical crack.

With smaller cracks it is usually best to try to place the outside edge of the toe of your boot into the crack. Keep your heel as low and as steady as possible as you move upwards. Moving your heel around is likely to decrease the effectiveness of the hold. On easier angled rock it is sometimes worth placing your foot with the toe downwards, and forcing the inside edge of the toe of your boot into the crack.

In larger cracks another type of foot placement could be called the 'heel and toe' foot jam. This is useful where the crack width is slightly less than the length of your foot. Place your toe slightly downwards and then force your heel downwards against the other side of the crack. This will jam your foot across the crack.

CRIMPS

Crimps are where the finger tips rest on tiny horizontal ledges on the rock surface. This is probably the most common type of hand hold used, as most of us would prefer to use a horizontal hold than a vertical one. The strongest crimp position is with your whole hand curled so your thumb is hooked slightly over the tip of your index finger. This is much stronger than curling your fingers over a hold alone with your hand in an open position. However, sometimes on sloping holds the open-handed position is better because it allows a greater surface area of skin to remain in contact with the rock.

Crimping is easily practised at home using a 'finger board' which is a training aid bolted to the wall. It is also possible to practise crimping on the door frames around the house. But if you try this be careful you don't pull them off.

SMEARS

Smears are another type of rather tenuous foothold. A smear is something less than a proper foothold. For example a very sloping foothold upon which you cannot get enough friction to support your whole bodyweight could be classified as a smear. It is better to use the smear and try to get some weight on it than ignore it completely. The rougher the rock surface the easier it will be to trust smears and put more of your bodyweight on your feet.

Practising climbing on smears is one way of increasing the strength of your arms and fingers because less weight is placed on your feet. However, you should nevertheless try to practise putting as much weight as possible on smears. It is often surprising just how much weight a smeared foothold can take. The ability to stand with nearly all of your weight on smears will

Hand crimped on a hold. Note how the knuckles are above the finger tips. Out of sight the thumb is hooked over the index finger for extra strength.

More weight can be put on the feet on very small holds than you may at first realise. These are called foot smears.

Slab climbing. (Etive Slabs)

greatly increase the efficiency of your climbing and will make you capable of much harder moves. This is because your fingers will be doing so much less of the work.

OFF-WIDTHS

The term off-width refers to crack widths, which are too wide for conventional jamming, but too narrow to get your whole body into for climbing as a chimney. Generally, off widths are climbed with one shoulder and one hip buried into the crack. Bending your arm will jam your shoulder into the crack, allowing you to move your feet up. In turn, bending your leg will jam your hip into the crack so your upper body can be moved upwards. Off width climbing is not everyone's favourite climbing technique, although it does have its aficionados, particularly in the USA where there is an abundance of off-width crack climbing.

Lay waying. (Skerryvore, Erraid)

With practice, you will find that even the most daunting rock face is manageable. (Rebublic of Scotland, Easter Island Buttress, Weem)

Summer Mountaineering

Moving away from roadside crags and into the mountains allows you to appreciate a whole range of new experiences. Firstly, the size and scale of routes are generally in a different league. The extra length of routes adds a number of new considerations. What is the best way down again? Is it better to walk down or abseil? Is there enough daylight to top out on the climb and get down again before dark? What retreat options are there should the route prove too exhausting? What will the wind and weather be like at the top of the climb? Should you carry walking boots to wear on the descent, or are you prepared to walk for miles in rock slippers? Do you need the map and compass to get off the top? Do you need extra clothing on the

Mountaineering brings a whole new range of climbing experiences.
(Aiguille Rouge, Chamonix Valley, France)

Mountain climbing can seem daunting at first, as it is more exposed, and you may well be climbing much higher than you are used to. (Caliban's Creep, Isle of Arran)

route? How much food and water will you need? Can you now still climb the route carrying a heavy rucksack?

The feeling of exposure is greatly enhanced on mountain crags, with thousands of feet of fresh air below your heels. These feelings of exposure can make the moves seem all the more difficult. What was a simple manoeuvre on the local crag now seems fraught with difficulty because of the extra thousand feet of space below you. Learning to control these feelings of exposure and climb well in such situations is a large part of the challenge and the satisfaction of climbing. Don't worry if the exposure preys on your mind during your first few routes in the mountains. You will gradually learn to deal with it through experience.

The weather too is likely to be less benign and more changeable in a mountain environment. Because of the need to be prepared for the climate it is usually necessary to carry some spare clothing on a mountain rock route. Therefore it is more likely that the climbing has to be done while wearing a rucksack. You may also have had a very long walk to your route of choice, perhaps of hours or even days, with an equally long return journey home once the climbing has been done. While the remoteness of the situation doubtless enhances the sense of adventure and achievement, it also adds greatly to the seriousness of the undertaking. The simplest of problems or injuries on a roadside crag can quickly become life-threatening in the mountains.

Guide book interpretation and route-finding may prove a little more difficult in the mountains than on smaller roadside crags. This can be even more daunting if you're in foreign lands and the guide book is not written in your native tongue. In addition, the consequences of straying off route are likely to be more punishing. One common mistake is to take only the route description for the route you intend to do, thus saving the weight of the whole guide book. However, events may not go to plan, and at the very least it is worth also carrying the descriptions for a few routes on either side of your intended course. These descriptions are also often useful in working out where you are when things get confusing. Also remember to copy out the description of possible descent routes from the top.

Alongside these considerations are the more basic skills necessary to operate successfully in a mountain environment. If you are good at surviving comfortably in the outdoors your mountain climbing adventures will be all the more pleasurable. Things like choosing the best camp or bivouac site, carrying the right amount of food and clothing, and being able to serve up good food for yourself and others, may sound obvious. But get just one of these factors wrong and you could be in for a miserable experience. Just being warm and dry, well-fed and comfortable in a remote mountain setting after a day's climbing is one of the most rewarding experiences there are. However, good survival skills do need to be learnt, and the best way is through experience.

On the bigger mountain routes, it is just as important to know what not to bring. Many potentially great ascents have turned into early retreats because the participants over-estimated the amount of food and equipment necessary. Just how frugal to be in your packing really depends upon the objective. For example if heading into a mountain crag for a few days to set up a base camp and climb from there, it is reasonable to take along a few luxury items and accept a few hours of heavy climbing. On the other hand, if leaving for an alpine ascent on a long route, which will require speed and endurance, your priority should be to pack as lightly as possible.

Climbing in mountains usually involves walking long distances uphill. Saving weight is certainly one way of making this task a lot easier, although knowing a little about how to walk uphill can also save a lot of energy. A common mistake is to walk up hills using the balls of the feet. This puts great strain on your calf muscles and uses many more muscles than necessary. A much better way to walk up hill keeps the heel firmly on the ground. This means that your calf muscles take much less strain. Instead the larger and more powerful muscles of your thighs and buttocks do the majority of the work. It may be necessary to work on the suppleness of the backs of your legs in order to be able to place your heel on the ground, with the toe pointed uphill. However, the effort will be worth it in terms of the energy saved later and the extra efficiency gained.

The peoples of the Himalayas have an incredibly efficient and graceful walking technique. While walking uphill their heel is kept firmly placed on the ground as their leg lifts the weight of their body. As their other foot is placed forward it is given a split second to rest before the weight of their body is rocked onto it. This calm and controlled method of walking has developed to allow them to carry heavy loads uphill all day (and day after day) without over-tiring any one muscle group and without damaging their tendons or joints.

Strength and stamina are even more important when cragging.
(Straw Donkey, El Churro, Spain)

Scrambling

The term 'scrambling' refers to the overlap between hill walking and climbing. At some point hill-walking terrain becomes steep and rocky enough to warrant using your hands. This is scrambling. The holds are big enough and the angle not steep enough, to warrant the use of a rope. The scrambler is, however, fairly committed to his or her objective. Retreat is not likely to be an easy option. Good route-finding is absolutely essential, since there may be no option to abseil should things go wrong. In many ways scrambling is a great introductory stepping stone into the wider world of mountaineering. It requires almost all of the skills necessary to operate successfully in the mountains, such as navigation, route finding, survival, basic climbing skills and nerve. The only thing missing is the rope. As such, scrambling is a great way into mountaineering for those with some hill-walking behind them but who do not wish to become involved with the use of ropes and protection. The lightweight approach and the time saved by not using any ropes or protection makes scrambling an extremely fast method of ascent. It can also be done alone as a climbing partner while advised, is not absolutely necessary.

However, without the back-up of a rope, good judgement in terms of the choice of route in the prevailing weather conditions, guide book interpretation and route finding are all absolutely vital. The standard of climbing must always be easy enough to reverse every move should the necessity arise.

Hazards to look out for include stone falls, loose or friable rock. In the early days of mountaineering many pioneers chose the line of gullies for their ascents. These had the advantage of protecting the climber from the exposure of the mountainside and could often be bridged-up using the walls on either side. However, gullies do tend to collect loose debris from above and so can be difficult to climb without dislodging stones. For this

Scrambling on A'Chir, Isle of Arran, Scotland

Scrambling on the stunning Caval Bernat ridge above Porto Pollensa in the north-west of Mallorca.

reason it is not a good idea to follow another party up a gully route. It is better to either get there early in the morning, or choose a cleaner buttress route instead.

One of the best areas of the world for scrambling is the Black Cuillin Mountains on the Isle of Skye, situated off the West Coast of Scotland. These small but majestic mountains offer almost limitless potential for scrambling. Good guide book interpretation and route-finding judgement are of paramount importance, especially so because the compass is unreliable in the Cuillin due to the magnetic properties of the rock. A complete traverse of the ridge provides a magnificent expedition although you will need a rope and a harness to abseil some

sections. Those who find success in traversing the whole ridge have usually taken the time to reconnoitre the ridge in order to gain some prior knowledge of the route. As the route takes an average twelve to fourteen hours to complete, it is necessary to carry plenty of food and water. Some parties choose to carry bivouac gear and make the traverse over two days, while others go lightweight and complete the route in one long day.

Navigation

MAP READING

Good navigation is an essential skill for any mountaineer. Fundamental to navigation is the ability to read a map and to be able to equate the map with the ground features and vice versa. A very common mistake in the beginning is to place too much emphasis on your compass while ignoring the ground features and your map. The compass can set you off in the right direction, but only the map can tell you where you are.

Therefore the first thing to learn is to read the map. Being able to equate shapes in the ground with the contours of the map is the key to map reading. When visibility is very poor it is still often possible to locate yourself on the map from just the slightest detail from the ground features. The more times you equate shapes in contours and the subtle changes in the spaces between the contours with the ground around you, the better your understanding and interpretation of the map will be.

The first thing to learn is to keep the map oriented with the ground. North on the map should point to North on the ground. Keeping the map oriented with the ground means it is much easier to make that essential leap of logic between the lines on paper and the surrounding shapes in the ground. It is much easier to identify features from ground to map or vice versa when the map is in the same alignment as the ground.

A useful method of interpreting the contours of the map is to imagine them as shorelines. Each contour represents the line that the shore would take if the water level were raised to that height. If you can imagine how these shorelines would look from above then you can understand the map.

USING A COMPASS

Fortunately learning to use a compass is much easier than learning to interpret a map with the ground. There are three main parts to a compass. These are the base plate, which has the 'direction of travel' arrow at one end; the bevel, which is oil filled, has parallel lines on the base called the 'orienting lines' and a red 'orienting arrow' and the compass needle, which is free to turn and should always point to (magnetic) north.

By taking a compass bearing, we are simply measuring the angle of a particular direction from the direction of north. The compass is a protractor for measuring angles and

also helps to find that angle on the ground thanks to the magnetic needle.

To take a bearing from one point to another on the map, first guess roughly what your bearing is going to be just by glancing at the map. If your proposed objective lies off to the Northeast the bearing should be between 0° and 90°. The reason we guess the angle first is because it is easy to make a 180° error while taking the bearing. If the figure we get after taking the bearing is radically different from our guessed angle it is a sure sign that a mistake has been made.

Use the edge of the compass to make a line through the point where you are located on the map, and through the point to which you wish to travel. Make sure that the direction of travel arrow is pointing towards the point you want to get to. A common mistake is to line up the two points but forget ensure that the direction of travel arrow points in the right direction. This mistake is one reason for the classic 180° error. Once lined up, with the direction of travel arrow pointing towards your goal, clasp the compass firmly to the map with the thumb and fingers of one hand. With your other hand, turn the bevel to make the orienting lines in the bevel parallel with the North/South gridlines on the map. Again make sure that the orienting arrow points to North on the map. If not, you have a second source of the classic 180° error. Also make sure that the base plate did not move on the map while the bevel was turned. The bearing taken can now be read at the point where the

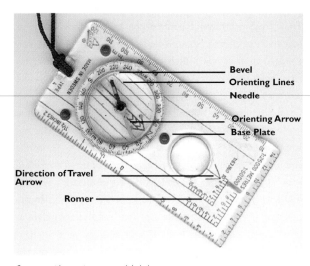

Compass with constituent parts labeled.

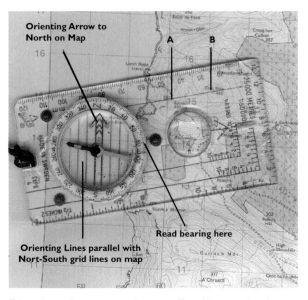

Orienting Arrow to
North on Map

16

A   B

16

Read bearing here

Orienting Lines parallel with
Nort-South grid lines on map

*Taking a bearing from a map using the compass. The red line passes through
point A where we wish to travel from, to point B, where we wish to travel to. The
direction of travel arrow points in the direction from A to B. With the base plate
clamped onto the map with thumb and fingers, the bevel has been turned so that
the orienting lines are parallel with the North-South grid lines on the map.*

direction of travel arrow touches the bevel. You must add on a
few degrees to allow for the variation between magnetic North
and grid North as given by the map. Remember you have
measured the angle to your objective by using grid North on the
map. However, when you come to walk there you will use
magnetic North as given by the compass needle. This small
difference, between grid North and magnetic North, needs to be
accounted for by adding on the 'magnetic variation'. Most
good maps will have the magnetic variation recorded
somewhere in the sheet margin. You will soon become familiar
with the magnetic variation for your area.

Taking the bearing from the map is only half the story. The other
major source of error you will encounter is while trying to walk
on the bearing, although there are ways to minimise this error.
First, hold the compass in front of your stomach, with the
direction of travel arrow pointing straight out away from you.
Gradually turn your whole body until the compass needle sits
inside the orienting arrow of the bevel. Make sure that the red
end of the needle (North) is inside the red end of the orienting
arrow. If you do this accurately, the direction of travel arrow will
now be pointing along the course to your proposed objective.
Rather than walking along trying to keep the needle inside the
orienting arrow, try instead to aim the compass accurately at
some object near to the limits of your visibility, be it a tuft of
grass or a rock. Then walk to that object and repeat the
exercise, aiming the compass at your next chosen object. Walking

on a bearing using this aiming technique is much more accurate
than just following the direction of travel arrow while trying to
keep the needle over the orienting arrow.

TIMING AND PACING

You can now go in the right direction. The other main element in
the art of not getting lost is to know how far you have
travelled. There are two main techniques for achieving this,
timing and pacing. First use the map to accurately measure the
distance of the proposed 'leg' of navigation. As a general rule
keep your chosen 'legs' of navigation as short as possible, as this
will tend to narrow down the accumulation of errors, and give
early warning if things are going wrong. You will need to be
familiar with the scale of maps for your area and the conversion
from millimetres to metres, or inches to miles.

Taking the timing technique first, you simply need to know the
average speed you are walking at, and use this to calculate the
estimated time it will take to walk your leg. Standard walking
speeds are usually 4km/h (2.5mph), 5 km/h (3mph) or rarely 6
km/h (3.5mph). At 4 km/h it takes 1.5 minutes to walk 100 metres
(320 feet), at 5km/h it takes 1.2 minutes to walk 100 metres
and at 6km/h it takes 1 minute to walk 100 metres.
The most frequent pace used is 5km/h. In our example, if the
leg was fairly flat, 700 metres (765 yards) would take 8.4 minutes.

Learning navigation techniques – particularly in winter – is essential.

Following a linear feature such as a gully is a useful navigation technique.

If you have a digital stopwatch on your wrist, start the timer as you start walking. Stop the watch if you stop for a rest along your route, and remember to start it again when you resume walking. If you have walked at a steady pace you will be surprised how accurate this technique can be.

Of course it is necessary to make allowance for uphill sections as they will doubtless take longer. This is easy if using maps where the contour interval (the vertical height between each contour) is 10 metres (32 feet). Simply add on one extra minute for each contour of ascent along the proposed route. In our example, if there are five contours of ascent over our 700 metre leg, we add 5 minutes to the 8.4 minutes we had calculated for the horizontal distance, thus giving 13.4 minutes as our final estimate. If you try this technique you will notice that it is necessary to walk at a very steady pace on the ascent. Allowing one minute for each 10 metre of ascent means that you can walk uphill without getting out of breath or breaking sweat. If you wish to go faster than   this pace it will be necessary to add one minute per contour for a proportion of the number of contours of ascent. Sometimes it is also necessary to add on time for steep descents, or for rough ground such as boulder fields. Only plenty of practice can give you the experience to use techniques such as this with confidence and accuracy.

Another technique for measuring the distance travelled is the use of pacing. To use this technique you first need to know the number of double paces (two steps) you take to every 100 metres (320 feet). As a guide, an adult male of average height may take roughly 62 double paces to 100 metres. However, you do need to know your own individual figure for this. Simply measure out 100 metres accurately, and then walk the distance in your normal walking gait, counting the number of double paces you take. When you come to use this on the mountain there may be adjustments to make for rough ground or deep snow, however when you are good at it, pacing can be incredibly accurate. In our example leg of 700m, rather than multiply 7 (hundred metres) by 62 (double paces), simply walk 62 double paces seven times, using your fingers or beads on your compass string to keep track of the number of hundreds passed.

OTHER NAVIGATIONAL TECHNIQUES

A few other navigational techniques are worth mentioning. The first is hand railing, which simply means following a linear feature such as a river or ridge to lead you towards your objective. Hand railing is simply making best use of the features on the map and the ground to plot a route. Occasionally the situation arises where you are heading for a particular point on a river or other linear feature. For example, imagine that it is dark or very misty and you have taken a compass bearing for a bridge over a large river. The slight inaccuracies of taking and walking on the bearing mean that you arrive at the river and no bridge is in sight. You are now faced with the agonising decision of which way to turn to look for the bridge. If, however, instead of aiming directly for the bridge you had aimed a little off, say upstream from the bridge, on arriving at the river bank you will then know to turn downstream. It is in instances such as these that the technique of aiming off is particularly valuable. Aiming off allows you to know which way to turn to find a particular point on a linear feature.

A good technique to help to locate yourself on the map uses the aspect of slope. This is useful if you are not sure which side of a hill or valley you are on. Simply aim the direction of travel arrow on the compass directly down the slope as accurately as possible. Turn the bevel so that the red orienting arrow falls directly beneath the needle. Check again that the direction of travel arrow still points straight down the hillside. You now need to subtract the magnetic variation from the magnetic bearing taken. Place the compass on the map and turn the whole base plate until the orienting lines in the bevel are parallel with the North South grid lines on the map (making sure that the red orienting needle points to North on the map). Now remember that the direction of travel arrow is pointing straight down the slope you are on. So on the map you must be on a slope where the contour lines are exactly perpendicular to the direction of

travel arrow (or the edge of the compass). In this way you can work out which side of a hill or valley you are on.

GETTING LOST

Inevitably, you will sometimes get a little lost when navigating in difficult conditions. The important thing is to be able to relocate yourself quickly and easily. To do this you need a strategy. Think through the possible places or areas of the map where you could conceivably be, given the aspect of slope you are on and any other evidence you have, such as the last identifiable feature you saw and the distance and direction travelled since then. Work out the best direction to head in which will take you to an identifiable point such as a summit or stream junction.

On every leg of navigation you should make a mental note of the features and slopes you expect to encounter given by the contour lines and any other information on the map before you start walking. Then as you walk you can tick off these features or subtle changes in slope angle etc. If the things you encounter are not quite what you had expected then this should serve as early warning that perhaps things are starting to go wrong. Therefore it is good practise to describe the proposed leg ahead in detail before beginning to walk. This will let you know more quickly that you are beginning to get lost rather than waiting until you are completely lost.

Students learning to navigate in the Galloway Hills.

Climbing on Snow and Ice

INTRODUCTION

So far this book has described the skills, techniques and equipment necessary to climb in summer conditions, i.e. in the absence of snow and ice. This section looks at the extra skills and equipment required for walking and climbing in colder conditions, where snow, sleet, ice, wind and severe cold can all have their impact on the mountain experience. Alongside the extra climbing protection utilised in snow and ice conditions a number of other factors necessary for success in such activities will be examined. Successful snow and ice climbing relies heavily on good survival skills, including the vital selection and use of clothing and equipment. In addition it is also essential to know and have practised the techniques for overnight survival in the snow, including the excavation or construction of snow shelters. The different types of snow and avalanche risk assessment are also discussed.

Whereas summer rock climbing in its purest form is very much tool-free, snow and ice climbing tends to rely heavily on the use of equipment. By practising the techniques described in the first part of this book, and under expert guidance, you may now feel comfortable moving over dry rock using your bare hands. However, the first time you don large mittens and take up an ice axe and crampons, you may well imagine that climbing fluently will not be easy. At first the tools used in snow and ice climbing appear fairly daunting. They are heavy, sharp and

The views when climbing in the snow and ice can be spectacular. (Nepal Himalayas)

cumbersome to use. However, with use and practise, winter climbing tools become like extensions of the human body.

The beauty of mountaineering in winter conditions relates to its continual freshness. Each storm wipes away all but the tiniest evidence that anyone has ever climbed there before. Snow covers the paths which trail through the mountains in summer time, and so turn overused tracks back into unexplored wilderness. The beauty of the pastime also stems from its seriousness, and it is important to understand just how serious all winter climbs really are. Any simple delay or navigational error can quickly become a life-threatening situation. Dark falls quickly in winter and the temperature generally plummets with the onset of darkness. Surviving an enforced unplanned bivouac will generally take guile and physical and emotional strength. Therefore try never to forget, even in the most beautiful weather, that a simple mistake could quickly become a very difficult situation. Be careful at all times. A sprained ankle in summer may mean a late arrival home. In winter it could mean the difference between life and death.

The distinction between climbing and walking in the winter or alpine mountaineering context is less clear than for summer climbing. At some indefinable point a walk up a steep snow slope

Climbing in snow and ice requires a whole range of new techniques, equipment and skills. (Prore, Coire an Lochain, Scotland)

Above: Climbing with experienced climbers is the best way to learn snow-ice skills.

Right: Topping out on a snow gully in Glen Coe, Scotland.

becomes a climb. In addition, the dangers of simply being in the mountain environment in winter conditions (or on alpine glaciers in summer) mean that the mountain walker and the mountain climber share similar attributes. Both require a number of specialist skills in terms of navigation, survival and the ability to read snow conditions. However, the climber also needs a few extra skills and these relate to the use of climbing axes, crampons, protection and the rope in snow-ice conditions.

Climbing in snow-ice conditions encompasses a wide range of styles and types of terrain. These include broad snow gullies, steep snow-ice gullies, waterfall ice, frozen turf, mixed climbing (including the ascent of snowed-up rock) and dry tooling. It is also necessary to take into account that the climbing conditions are changing all the time. Each day (and sometimes each hour) the route will be different. Temperature changes mean that a reasonable ice climb in the morning may become a thawing mess just an hour or two later. Equally, a difficult hoar-frosted mixed route could melt in the sun and become more like an easy summer rock climb within the space of a few hours.

Therefore it is clearly important to gain a good understanding of the interaction between the weather, and its effects on climbing conditions. Talking to local climbers is an essential first step in understanding this relationship. Over time you will learn to predict with some degree of accuracy what climbing conditions may be like on a given day from the weather patterns and the forecast. A freeze-thaw cycle in the mountains can produce excellent snow-ice climbing conditions; a large fall of powder snow may rule out a technical mixed climb; a short period of freezing weather may not have been sufficient to freeze the turf making your proposed objective positively dangerous.

The special skills involved in ascending each of these types of terrain are described in the next section. It must be stressed, however, that there is no substitute for qualified instruction, and climbing with an experienced partner is the best way to learn these skills.

Alpine/Winter Mountaineering Equipment

Preparing for snow-ice conditions requires an extensive array of equipment, and you may find selecting equipment difficult when you begin. For example, a pair of technical climbing axes may seem like a desirable purchase, but a longer shafted walking axe is a better choice for a beginner. Although this axe may become redundant once you leave the gentle snow gullies for the steep ice or the turf buttresses, it is nevertheless the right choice in the beginning. Similarly, the choice between mittens and gloves and your selection of boots and crampons may depend upon how technical a climber you are aiming to be.

Enduring mountain snow-ice conditions generally requires some expensive clothing, and even this can call for some modification in the worst conditions. You may find that the most stylish jackets and salopettes are inadequate in certain conditions.

Try to keep your initial purchase to the essential minimum, as, seduced by the latest gimmickry, many novice climbers find themselves weighed down by unnecessary equipment. Make sure you understand clearly the disadvantages of using high-tech climbing tools over traditional ones as this could make a vital difference in many situations.

CLOTHING

The right clothing for the winter mountain environment is vital. If you are uncomfortable, the experience is unlikely to be enjoyable, and could be lethal. It is also important to understand how best to use the clothing. This means avoiding getting soaked with sweat when your body is working hard, yet wrapping up quickly as soon as you stop. For this reason clothing with underarm zips is often preferred. Such clothing can be adjusted quickly to allow the escape of heat and vapour when working, yet is quickly readjusted to prevent heat loss when resting. This avoids the constant donning and removal of layers. However, it is essential to make sure the zips are fully closed in the worst conditions, and zips should be kept in good repair, as a burst zip could be disastrous.

Avoiding becoming soaked with sweat is one of the most difficult problems in relation to clothing. The effort expended in transporting a heavy rucksack containing ropes, climbing gear, axes and crampons uphill through deep snow can be immense. Working this hard means that the body soon overheats and produces large quantities of cooling sweat. It is essential to avoid soaking too many of those vital insulatory layers of clothing. For this reason mountaineers often use the layering system.

The first layer generally consists of thermal underwear, made of nylon or polyester. Avoid cotton as it quickly becomes soaked in sweat and does not dry out easily. Most people use thermals

Learning what not to take ia as important as knowing what is needed when climbing in snow and ice.

made of manmade fibres instead, which have a high wicking capacity. The ability of this layer to wick moisture away from the skin is important. It must be a fabric which dries out nearly as quickly as it gets wet.

On top of a thermal layer most people wear fleece. Fleece is another manmade fibre and mainly a by-product of the oil industry, although some fleece material is recycled from plastic bottles. Fleece is designed to trap air and so provides an insulatory layer between the thermals and the outer shell. However, most fleece garments are not windproof. As such, they can be totally ineffectual in a cold wind without a shell windproof layer on top. It is possible to buy fleece garments with a windproof, and even a showerproof, layer integral to the fabric. These new fleeces may be more versatile, but for snow-ice conditions a separate outer wind and waterproof shell is still recommended.

Salopettes and jackets made from breathable waterproof membrane fabrics are normally worn in snow and ice.

Goretex appears to be the most widely adopted type of fabric used in shell (outer-layer) garments. This was the first fabric of which it was claimed that it was waterproof, and 'breathable', although a number of other fabrics making this same claim are now available. Waxed cotton was the original fabric used in breathable waterproof shell garments. These had the advantage of being very durable in comparison to many of the more modern fabrics, but suffered the disadvantage of being somewhat heavier. Waxed cotton clothing may be making a return to the climbing scene with the reintroduction of new lightweight waxed cotton fabrics. The extra durability of waxed cotton over other manmade fabrics makes them well worth considering.

Something to look out for in shell garments is an abundance of large pockets for map and map case, compass, gloves, snacks etc. You will also need a large enough hood to accommodate your climbing helmet. Beware of removable hoods as strong winds have a tendency to snatch them away. Velcro too can be rendered useless by becoming wet and then freezing, so beware of garments with an over-reliance on Velcro. Make sure there is plenty of room inside the coat to allow free movement of the arms, and ensure that it can be sealed at the waist, wrists and neck.

Salopettes are useful because they insulate the back and kidneys while climbing. They prevent a gap forming between the upper body garments and those of the lower body with the constant reaching and stretching involved in climbing. Make sure with legwear that you can still make high steps and wide bridging moves without constriction. Suppleness is just as important in snow-ice climbing as it is on rock.

The choice of boots again depends partly on where you see yourself going. Winter walking boots may bend slightly and have a greater 'rocker' on the sole than a purely technical climbing boot. Technical climbing boots may have a flatter sole and are unlikely to bend at all. This makes walking more difficult, although they have the advantage that there is no 'give' in the boot when standing only on the front points of the crampons (i.e. on very steep ground). A plastic boot, with enough rocker on the sole to make walking comfortable, yet stiff enough to stand on front points alone without flexing is a good compromise. Remember that however hard you intend to climb you are still likely to do a considerable amount of simple walking, although walking on snow is a lot more comfortable than walking on a hard surface when wearing plastic boots. It is probably a good idea to choose crampons and boots at the same

New lightweight breathable waterproof materials are becoming more popular. They depend upon a fine wax layer to keep the water out and imitate animal fur.

Like boots and axes, your choice of gloves will be affected by your aspirations. Woollen Dachstein mittens are best for winter walking and easier grade snow and ice routes. It is certainly worth having a pair whatever you intend to do, even if only as a spare pair. They are inexpensive and very durable and effective. Gloves, on the other hand, tend to be the opposite   expensive, not very durable and less effective than mittens at keeping hands warm. Gloves are, however, more useful on harder grade routes, making it easier to place protection and tie knots. A spare set of gloves or mittens is advisable as they are easily lost. Idiot loops (strings which attach the gloves or mittens to your other garments) are also a good idea.

If you have ever suffered from 'the hot aches' you will appreciate the importance of good gloves or mittens. The hot aches occur after the hands have become numb with cold. As warm blood rushes back into your hands, the pain can be excruciating to the point of nausea. The best you can do in this situation is to remember that the pain only lasts a few minutes and will go away again soon. Some people experience hot aches more than others and this has a lot to do with circulation to the extremities. Try to avoid caffeine and nicotine, as these are vaso-constrictors, which tend to reduce blood flow to the extremities.

A warm balaclava or fleece hood is another necessity for snow and ice climbing. As much as 40% of the body's heat is lost through the head and neck alone. Make sure that the fabric is not so thick as to prevent it from being worn under the helmet.

In some conditions sunglasses are necessary to prevent snowblindness, a painful condition caused by the entry of too much light to the eyes. If you experience illusory colours or pain in the eyes in bright conditions take immediate steps to reduce the amount of light entering your eyes.

THE ICE AXE

The ice axe is perhaps the piece of mountaineering equipment to which a climber can become most attached. It is held in the hand for much of the time; prevents a short slide turning into a lethal fall; can cut steps out of hard ice, and when swung into good turf or snow ice it can provide a feeling of security not found in summer rock climbing. The ice axe can become a trusted friend.

Axes are of two main types, general mountaineering axes and technical climbing axes. It is undoubtedly best to start off with a general mountaineering axe (sometimes called a walking axe).

time. Some leather boots can only be used with strap-on crampons. If you want to use quick fitting step-in crampons, make sure you acquire suitable boots. Usually this means boots with a rigid sole and a sufficient welt at the toe and heel to hold the wire binding of the step-in crampon.

Gaiters are necessary anywhere you are likely to encounter snow. Otherwise snow gets inside the boot. This will either soak the boots as the snow melts, or may form a painful ring of ice around the ankle. The gaiters must endure their close proximity to the metal points of the crampons and the battering they receive from the rocks. Tough cheap gaffers can often be the best choice.

An ice axe ia an essential piece of equipment.

clearance on modern technical ice tools must be considered a serious drawback. Self-arrest with technical climbing tools is less effective and requires a good deal more skill.

The longer shaft and large right-angled adze of the walking axe make it much more useful for cutting steps in ice. Learning to cut steps in ice is more than mere tradition. It is a very useful skill to have. When you lose or break a crampon the only safe way to proceed may be by cutting steps.

Technical climbing axes tend to have steeply angled picks, which are usually reverse-curved with negative clearance. This makes them more secure on steeper ice and turf. The shaft of technical axes tends to be shorter as they are more often swung than their walking counterparts. As they are shorter and often have steeply angled adzes, it can be difficult to cut steps with a technical axe. In addition, ice axe an boot belays will be less secure because of the shorter shaft. Above all, if you have learned to self-arrest with a more traditional axe, make sure you practise the skill again on an icy snow slope with a safe run-out with your new technical tool. Try the two types of axe alternately to see how much more difficult self-arrest is with the technical tool.

A good quality wrist loop is essential on any ice axe. You should be able to move your hand in and out of the wrist loop easily, but it should not be able to slip off unexpectedly. Dropping an axe on a difficult pitch must be every climber's nightmare. Make sure that the tape forming the wrist loops is broad enough to be comfortable.

Technical mixed climbing puts enormous demands on ice tools. Ice picks are often twisted (or torqued) into cracks and pulled on in ways which were not foreseen by the tool's original designer. The properties of the metal used also become critical for this type of climbing. Too soft and it will bend, too hard and the metal can break under strain.

CRAMPONS

Your choice of crampons is best made in line with your choice of boots. If you go for fairly flexible leather boots, you may have no choice but to opt for flexible strap-on crampons. If you have stiff plastic boots with a suitable welt at the heel and toe you will have the option of choosing step-in crampons.

Anyone who has tried to fit strap-on crampons in a freezing blizzard will appreciate the beauty of the quick fitting step-in. They are also much quicker to remove again which can save

These axes often have a slightly longer shaft, making them more secure when the spike is driven into the snow. The pick on a walking axe tends to project from the shaft at about 90° and then droops downwards. The point of the pick on a walking axe may be either positive clearance or negative clearance. With positive clearance the top edge of the pick forms the protruding point of the axe. The advantage is that this type of axe is smoother and easier to use for self-arrest. Negative clearance axes, where the protruding point is formed by the lower edge of the pick, may be more secure on steep ground, but they tend to be less predictable in self-arrest situations. The protruding point is more likely to snag suddenly, pulling the axe out of your hands, or bounce out unexpectedly. As self-arrest is one of the most important functions of the axe, negative

Crampons should be chosen to fit your boots and requirements.

precious moments near the end of a day's climbing. However, step-in crampons can be more problematic than their strap-on cousins. If the wire toe bail falls off half way up a route, you are going to have to be pretty ingenious to get out of the situation. With strap-on crampons you can simply fit a spare strap and start again. Some step-in crampons do come with rings for fitting a strap as a backup and these may be worth considering. Either way it is worth getting good quality crampons. Make certain too that they fit your boots properly, and are not too tight on the boot, as this can bend the plastic and make the boot uncomfortable.

If you intend to specialise in one or other type of winter climbing, this may also affect you choice of crampon. Ice climbing requires fairly long sharp front points, which will embed deeply into the medium. For mixed climbing, or snowed-up rock climbs, many people prefer crampons with shorter points, which put less strain on the ankles when standing on small rock holds. The snow types most commonly found in your area may also affect the best choice of crampon. If temperatures are generally around or just above freezing, the snow is likely to be mushy or sticky. In this case it may be worth avoiding crampons which have vertical sides as these may be more prone to 'ball-up' with snow. Such 'balling-up' can be a nuisance and also dangerous, as when you step forward, rather than placing metal spikes in the snow you find yourself placing a great ball of mushy snow ahead instead. The usual technique for removing balled-up snow from a crampon involves tapping the boot with the shaft of the axe as the boot is lifted out of the snow. The knock is usually enough to dislodge the stuck snow. Balling up can also be negated to some extent by the use of anti-balling plates or simply gaffer tape wrapped around the crampon. Anti-balling plates work by pushing the clogged snow out of the crampon. The gaffer tape method simply makes the crampon less prone to hold the snow.

OTHER EQUIPMENT

The other essential equipment you will require is a head torch, unless perhaps the only snow-ice climbing you will do is inside the Arctic circle in summer time. If the falling of darkness is in any way a possibility, make sure you carry a head torch with a fresh battery. Make sure you know this piece of equipment inside out. You will probably have to repair it in the dark at some point, or at the very least replace a bulb. The head torch must be water-proof and durable. You should also ensure that the head

torch can be fitted properly to your climbing helmet. You may need to fit some shock cord to your helmet. You may also need to re-adjust the straps on the torch to fit over the helmet. Make sure you have prepared yourself for finishing your climb in the dark. Particularly in the beginning, the time taken on winter routes is likely to be well above any time given in the guide book, or your expectations.

You must also carry the most basic means for overnight survival. This may be a small down jacket stuffed into a waterproof bag and a cheap plastic bivouac bag. In addition, it is well worth carrying a little extra food in case you are benighted. There is an old climbing dictum which states that if you carry bivouac gear you will end up having to use it. If you weight yourself down with every possible piece of equipment, this may well be the case. It is better to carry only the basics, which will weigh very little in total. Remember too that a cheap plastic bivouac bag is likely to be warmer than an expensive breathable model. This is precisely because plastic does not breathe; with vapour loss there is also heat loss.

Carrying all the necessary equipment can be cumbersome, so use lightweight varieties wherever possible. (The Cardinal, Ben a Bhuird)

Conditions can change rapidly in the mountains.(Tour Glacier, French Alps)

Also essential is some kind of insulated drinking vessel, which won't turn your juice into solid ice. Unbreakable flasks are popular, but many choose simply to get by with a lighter and cheaper plastic bottle. You may at some stage wish to try a planned bivouac in winter conditions. As the best shelter in winter is a snow hole, you will require a snow shovel. Some lightweight plastic snow shovels will shatter on first impact with icy snow, while some aluminium varieties will need modification to prevent them falling to pieces with use. Therefore, while being aware of the need to save on weight, try also to remember that this piece of equipment needs to be strong.

You will also need to carry a first-aid kit, details of which are covered at the end of the book. By the time you pack your winter climbing sack with rope, protection, harness, helmet, crampons, first aid kit, bivouac bag, spare food, spare clothing, lunch, flask, outer shell garments, head torch, gloves, spare gloves, balaclava and perhaps a camera, with two climbing axes strapped to the outside, you may be wondering how you are going to make it to the foot of the crag. The best advice is to buy lightweight versions of each item where possible. For example, a titanium flask, frame-less rucksack, small camera etc. In any case you will need to be very fit to climb well in winter conditions. A couple of hours a week running and pushing leg weights can make a huge difference to the apparent effort required to walk in to the climbing routes at the weekend.

Alpine/Winter Climbing Skills

A whole new range of skills and techniques is necessary to master the use of your new ice toolsand the snow-ice medium. These include moving around on crampons, kicking steps, cuttingsteps and stances, using the axe for security, self-arrest, snow and ice belays, and the excavation of snow shelters. If you are going to practise any of the techniques described in this chapter, do so in the company of experienced climbers. Choose an area of slope with a safe 'run-out' and an absence of protruding rocks and boulders. This way if you make a mistake, the consequences won't be too serious.

USING THE AXE

The axe is your most important tool, as you must be able to protect yourself from falling and sliding before moving on to learn other techniques. On moderate snow slopes, the most common position to hold an ice axe is by the head with the spike pointing downwards. The pick may point either forwards or backwards. Having the pick pointing backwards is often preferred, as the axe is already the right way round to halt a slide. On very steep snow it may be more useful to point the pick forwards as it will also bury into the slope, providing extra protection. Either way, on suitable slopes the spike can be driven down into the snow to provide security. If a slip occurs, pressing down on the head of the axe should drive the shaft even further into the snow and stop the slide immediately. When using the spike and shaft in this way it is important that the shaft is driven vertically downwards into the snow. Driving the shaft in perpendicular to the slope will be much less effective as it could slide out more easily in the event of a slip.

SELF-ARREST

Self-arrest, or ice-axe braking as it is commonly known, is a technique used to stop a slide on a snow or ice slope. If you are going to practise self- arrest, which involves halting a slide from a variety of positions, you will need to wear a waterproof outer shell layer to avoid getting soaked. However, do not use your best breathable coat and salopettes for this purpose. Snow can have sharp rime crystals on the surface, which will perforate and destroy such expensive clothing. If you can, use an old waterproof neoprene coat and trousers to practise basic ice axe skills and keep some spare dry clothes in your rucksack. Practise ice-axe

Knowledge and experience of glaciers is essential for alpine climbing. Note rope coils around climber, and rope in case of crevasse.

braking with one axe, and without rucksack or crampons. You should, however, wear your helmet and gloves for protection at all times.

If you can, practise these techniques first using a general mountaineering axe, preferably with positive clearance at the tip of the pick. This will allow you to get a better feel for how an axe should be used to arrest a slide than by using a technical climbing axe. Once the basic skills have been mastered you can try again with a technical axe to discover how much more difficult it is to come to a controlled stop.

Kick or cut yourself a small stance in the snow on a snow slope steep enough to slide on, but not so steep that you will tumble. Remember to choose a slope with a safe run-out at the bottom so that if your braking fails you will not get injured. Run though each of these techniques in your head before trying them out for real. The first position to learn is face down, legs downhill. This is the position that you will need to get into to arrest a fall from

Self-arrest – feet first.

any other position. The procedures are outlined here on one side only, although you will need to be able to carry them out competently on both sides.

Begin by holding the head of the axe in your right hand with the pick pointing backwards. Bring the head of the axe up to just under your right shoulder. The adze should now be towards your shoulder and the pick pointing outwards. The left hand should hold the spike close to your abdomen on your left-hand side and should cover the spike to prevent it becoming snagged in the snow. The shaft of the axe should lie diagonally across your chest.

As you slide, keep your feet from touching the surface of the snow at all times. This is vital, as you will need to be able to execute this technique wearing crampons. During a slide, if the front points come into contact with the icy surface of the snow, the resultant snag can cause you to go into a terrifying tumble instead. Better to learn not to let your feet touch the snow in the first place.

As you begin to slide down the slope knees first, draw the axe close to your chest and keep the head of the axe just below your right shoulder. In a controlled way, hunch your bodyweight over the head of the axe, burying the pick gradually deeper into the snow. The front of your helmet should be scraping the surface of the snow, while your elbows should not be in contact with the snow. It is important to keep the axe locked in position with your arms and to use your whole torso to place the pick firmly in a controlled fashion into the snow to arrest the slide. If you use your arms to place the pick instead, you are in danger of having the axe ripped from your hands should the pick suddenly snag in the icy surface.

You should also learn to arrest a fall from a variety of other positions. To remedy a slide head first downhill on your front, place the head of the axe out at arms length from the body, keeping hold of the spike with the other hand. Drive the pick into the snow as far from your body as possible. This will cause your body to swing round so that your legs are now downhill. Once in this position repeat the procedure for braking described previously. To get out of a slide on your back with your feet downhill you will need to roll over onto your front. However, you must roll

WALKING TECHNIQUES

Walking techniques on snow differ greatly from walking without snow. Rather than choosing a place for your foot, you will instead kick your own foot placement (unless the snow is so hard that this is not possible). When ascending reasonably angled snow slopes it is best to zig-zag from side to side rather than heading straight up the slope. This allows you to use the edge of your boot to kick each step in the snow and makes it easier to get weight on the heel. To kick a step across the slope in this way, swing the boot from the knee and use the edge of the boot to saw into the snow slope. This will require little effort as you are using the momentum of the boot, and the serration on the edge of the sole to cut into the snow. Step through with the other foot, this time using the inside edge of the boot to saw the step. Each step made in this way should be horizontal across the slope. Together these holds should form a diagonal line across the slope. As the slope angle steepens it eventually becomes necessary to face into the slope kicking the toes of the boots straight into the slope. This means that ascent is directly up the slope rather than from side to side.

Self- arrest. – on your front – head downhill.

towards the side of your body which is holding the head of the axe, so that the pick can be placed in a controlled fashion when back on your front. Rolling in the other direction will cause the pick to suddenly bury itself in the snow as you tumble over. This could cause the pick to be ripped from your grip if it catches in an icy surface. You must also remember to keep you boots off the surface of the snow at all times. Otherwise there could be nasty consequences when you come to try it wearing crampons.

Finally, there is the 'head downhill on your back' sliding position. To extricate yourself from this predicament, hold the head of the axe in your right hand with the left hand covering the spike. Place the pick into the snow by your right hand side while raising your head towards the right. Bearing down slightly on the head of the axe will allow your hips to swing down to a position below the head of the axe. As you swing round, also roll over so that you end up on your front with your legs downhill as before. Remember to do this without allowing your boots to touch the snow.

Self- arrest.– on your back – feet downhill, keep feet up.

Cutting steps on Angel's Peak in the Cairngorms

In hard snow the foot ledge may be narrower or shallower than the boot sole. This should not matter provided you have good balance and know how to use your axe. When the surface of the snow-ice is too hard to saw an adequate foot placement, it becomes necessary either to cut steps with the adze, or wear crampons.

CUTTING STEPS

Cutting steps into snow-ice using the adze is part of the great tradition of mountaineering, and is a vital technique to know today. Sometimes you will encounter a small area of snow-ice over which it will be quicker to cut steps than don crampons. Or you may lose or break a crampon, or be with someone else who has. Therefore it is important to be a good step cutter.

It is preferable to use a general mountaineering axe for learning to cut steps as this will be much easier. Choose an area of hard snow-ice with a safe run-out in case you slip. Stand sideways on the slope as when kicking steps with the side of the boot. Hold the axe at the bottom of the shaft on the side towards the slope. Turn the axe in your hand so that the adze is to the rear and the pick is to the front. Swing the axe with a straight arm so that the adze grazes the surface of the snow ice. The axe should leave a horizontal cut in the surface. When doing this, the axe should carry through in its swing. If the adze sticks, you are trying to cut too much at once, and will need more effort to remove the adze and swing again. Take a smaller slice with each swing if this happens and be prepared to take two or more swings to cut each foot placement. Once each step is cut, the lower foot can be moved up onto the new foot placement created, and the process repeated. Cutting steps down the slope is obviously more difficult as you have to reach below your feet with the adze to cut each step.

USING CRAMPONS

You should have adjusted your crampons to fit your boots in the comfort of your own home and practised their fitting and removal. Strap-on crampons are notoriously difficult to put on while wearing mittens or gloves, and are equally hard to put on with numb fingers. Step-ins have the advantage that they are quick to don, and with practise this can even be done with gloves on. The best position for fitting crampons to your boots is sitting with your foot placed up on a boulder. Failing this, at least sit down so that you don't topple over and slide down the slope without the axe to stop you. Make sure you have all straps fastened correctly. There is nothing worse than starting off up a route to discover that one, or both, crampons are not fastened properly. Trying to correct the problem half way up a pitch is more difficult, dangerous and time consuming than doing it right to start with.

As soon as you don crampons you can move in a different way, and can traverse hard ice without fear of slipping. When you use crampons, ensure that none of your clothing is flapping around your legs. Wide trousers, loose gaiters and even long straps on the rucksack can easily snag crampon points and cause an unexpected and perhaps serious trip. If necessary wear your trousers inside your gaiters so that there is nothing loose to snag

It is essential to understand the advantages of each different type of crampon.

sharp points. Also remember to walk (and climb) with your feet wider apart than usual. This will help prevent tripping, as well cuts in your gaiters, plastic boots and legs. Never place one foot on top of the other wearing crampons. Many a climber has done this and driven a point right through the other boot.

Choose an area of fairly easy angled hard snow-ice or water-ice to practise moving around in crampons for the first time. Place each foot positively so that the points of the crampons penetrate the ice. You may even stamp downwards slightly to provide a really firm foot placement. Moving over hard ice with crampons is very different from sawing steps without them. Rather than keeping the sole of the boot level, with crampons the sole of the boot is kept parallel with the slope. Using crampons will soon give you supple ankles. The steeper the ice you walk on with crampons, the more supple your ankles will need to be. Try walking across, up and down a gentle ice slope, at all times placing as many points as possible firmly into the ice by keeping the sole parallel to the surface. As you move, do not

let the boot rock around on the icy surface. The crampon points in the ice should not move at all until the other foot is firmly placed and your weight has been transferred onto it.

AVALANCHE RISK ASSESSMENT

Avalanches are not freak events in the mountains as some people imagine. If you climb for long enough in the snow and ice you will see or be caught in one soon enough. Not all avalanches are large enough to bury a victim, although in the wrong place even a small avalanche could cause a serious fall.

Therefore you will need to learn how to assess the risk of avalanche on any given snow slope on any particular day. Firstly, there are the obvious sources of information. Many climbing areas give out avalanche risk reports on a daily basis, either on the local radio station or by posting reports in prominent places. These are invaluable, as they will tend to localise and specify particular risk areas (for example, gullies facing north-east or perhaps even one particular slope, which is a known avalanche hot spot).

The second source of information is through your own analysis of the previous few days of weather. For example, a fall of fresh snow followed by gale force winds from the south-west is likely to create an avalanche risk in north-east facing gullies. This is because the fresh snow will be blown and re-deposited on the lee side of the mountains forming a snow pack called windslab. It is vital that you learn how to make your own decisions.

Thirdly, and perhaps most importantly, you will need to understand some basic principles about snow and the snow pack. The ancient peoples of Greenland allegedly had over one hundred names for snow, in all its various types, which shows just how many different variations of snow there are. The snow pack on any particular slope is usually made up of layers of different types of snow. One way to check the stability of these layers, and hence the risk of avalanche, is to dig a snow pit. You may not be able to check the full depth of the snow pack for weak layers, but you can quickly check the stability of the first couple of feet. To do this, dig a pit and create a smooth vertical wall on the uphill side of the pit. Look carefully at the layers exposed by this method. Each layer has a different thickness and hardness. Some may be ice hard while other layers are composed of powder. Particularly dangerous are sharp changes in

Zigzagging across the slope and kicking steps is the safest way of ascending.

the hardness of the layers. For example, very soft snow on top of a hard ice layer can mean a weakness exists in the snow pack. Also watch out for a layer of hailstones in the snow pack which can act like ball bearings in releasing the layers above it. With a pit you can easily test the stability of the snow pack by cutting a deep slot around an area above the pit. This slot leaves a block of the snow pack unsupported from above and below. If it slides off and lands in your snow pit without any assistance, you should perhaps leave the slope as quickly as possible. If not, place the shaft of an axe in the slot above the block and lever gently at first, gradually increasing the force on the block until it releases and slides into the pit. This procedure will give you a clear idea of how well attached the top layers are to those underneath.

Other factors you should be aware of include how the shape and angle of a slope affect the risk of an avalanche. Avalanches occur most frequently between 30° and 45°, although they can also occur outside this range. The risk of avalanche is much greater on convex slopes where there is likely to be some tension on the snow pack. Conversely, concave slopes where the snow pack will be under compression are much less likely to avalanche. Finally, there are some excellent books specifically about avalanches and their risks, which are well worth studying. They will also provide information on what to do if you are caught in an avalanche, and how to search for buried victims.

Flat footing on ice – adjust your stance according to the angle of terrain underfoot.

Alpine/Winter Walking

ALPINE/WINTER WALKING

This chapter considers use of the rope in winter mountaineering, and covers skills such as snow belays, ice axe belays and the construction of snow shelters. It also looks at more advanced navigation skills, as the presence of snow and ice means that the consequences of mistakes tend to be more serious. The vast majority of accidents in the hills and mountains stem from navigation errors. Therefore the better your mastery of these skills, the fewer opportunities there will be for unexpected benightment, falls or exhaustion hypothermia.

WINTER FITNESS

Nothing will leave you better prepared for winter mountaineering than a good base level of fitness. Such fitness allows you to escape quickly from bad weather or to relocate after a long detour in bad conditions. A fairly high level of fitness and endurance is also essential for your enjoyment, as this is a physically demanding pastime; the rucksack is heavy, the snow deep, the clothing bulky, and you may be carrying an axe for most of the day. Add potentially heat-sapping weather conditions and the need to concentrate on navigation and you will start to appreciate the need for a high level of fitness.

The type of fitness required for this type of winter mountaineering is quite different from that for summer rock climbing. As the whole body works hard for long periods on a winter day, the benefits of a strong and efficient cardio-vascular system cannot be underestimated. The usual way to acquire such cardio-vascular fitness is by running two or three times a week. As the winter season progresses and you get into the mountains with some frequency, you will notice an increase in your level of fitness. Therefore as with rock climbing, the best training for winter climbing, is winter climbing itself.

WINTER NAVIGATION

Winter navigation is fraught with extra difficulties. Firstly, many of the ground features shown on the map may no longer be visible on the ground. Even the shapes of these features may have changed due to the build-up of snow and may look different from their appearance on the map.

Additionally, the levels of visibility in winter can be appallingly low. So called 'white outs' occur when the air is so full of mist and snow that it is impossible to distinguish any ground features at all.

Good navigation is essential in bad conditions, here on Ben Alder in winter.

In these conditions on gentle slopes, it may be impossible to determine which way is up and which is down, or even if you are on a slope at all. For these reasons your navigational skills need considerable refinement to provide any degree of safety in winter conditions.

Extreme winter conditions require advanced skills. (Gastronome, Beinn Eighe)

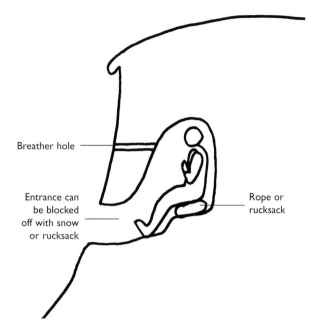

Breather hole

Entrance can
be blocked
off with snow
or rucksack

Rope or
rucksack

The presence of deep snow will obviously affect the time it takes to cover a given distance, and you will therefore need to adjust your time estimates. Pacing is affected by the depth of snow, which complicates the calculation of distance travelled. These are things which will take practise and personal experience to perfect.

It is arguably even more important to be accurate while taking and walking on compass bearings in winter conditions. Fortunately the snow provides opportunities to check the accuracy of your bearing. To do this, swing around 180 while walking on a bearing in the snow. Aim the direction of travel arrow exactly along the line of your tracks in the snow. If you have been walking on your bearing, the compass needle will lie exactly inside the orienting arrow, with the red end of the needle inside the black end of the orienting arrow (i.e. exactly 180° from the way it should be). If there is a slight deviation between your tracks and the bearing you have taken this will provide an early indication that you are going wrong.

Another useful technique in very bad visibility is the use of a front man marker. Rather than pointing the compass into the whiteness, you can use a member of your party to walk ahead within the limit of your visibility. Ask this person to move from side to side until they are in line with your compass bearing. As they move forward, continue to check with your compass that the direction of travel is accurate, and continue to shout instructions to keep them on line. This technique can be risky for the front person, especially if you are near corniced cliff tops. In

this situation rope the whole party together to prevent the untimely disappearance of the front person.

Because of the existence of cornices in winter it may be useful to learn to 'box' dangerous areas such as deeply incised head walls. Gullies can often cut deep into the summit areas of mountains and when disguised by cornices these areas can be particularly treacherous to traverse. Therefore, rather than skirt around the edge of a dangerous head wall or cliff top in bad visibility, it is possible to box the area instead. To do this, take a bearing to your desired final destination and measure the distance. Then either add or subtract 90° to travel away from the edge for a fixed distance, say 100 metres (328 feet). Then turn 90° to walk parallel with your original bearing and travel for the exact distance of the original leg. When done, turn 90° again and travel back towards your target, pacing out the exact distance travelled on the first side of the box in this example 100 metres.

Your choice of route is crucial in winter mountaineering. Often it is possible to take a slightly more devious route and avoid the need to lose and regain height, or perhaps avoid an area of deep snow.

SNOW AND ICE BELAYS

In many situations using a rope can greatly enhance your safety and security. For example, getting over a cornice can be dangerous without a rope, as can negotiating a steeper than expected snow slope. There is a great deal that can be done to make situations like these safer by using a rope alone. All forms of snow belay are inherently weaker than their solid rock counterparts. However, at the same time the forces generated on a snow belay are also likely to be lower, because they are expected to arrest slides on snow rather than vertical drops. Because they are weaker, it is better to use a more dynamic form of belaying so that the belay is subjected to lower forces. Therefore, a variety of forms of body belay are common in these situations. Such body belays are quick to establish and they can be executed more dynamically than with a belay device because it is easier to perform a controlled deceleration of the falling body.

The bucket seat is probably the most common form of snow belay. With the adze of your axe, dig a deep hole into the snow slope. Dig slots in the slope below this to accommodate each leg so that your heels can be dug into the surface. When you sit in this hole your bottom should be below your knees. If not you are in danger of being pulled from your seat in a fall.

Without a harness or waist belt, you and your climbing partner will need to tie into either end of the rope with a figure-of-eight knot or a bowline. The belayer sits deep in the bucket seat with heels firmly dug into the slope and casts the rope around his or her waist. As the climber ascends the rope is paid out. In the event of a slide it is important not to lock off the rope too tightly. Simply gripping the rope will be sufficient to decelerate the sliding climber. The friction generated by the rope running over the back of your jacket and through your gloved hands will be just about enough in itself to bring the sliding climber to a gradual halt. It is extremely good fun to practise this technique with a partner, but only do so on a slope with a safe run-out and in the presence of a qualified mountaineering instructor.

SNOW SHELTERS

Snow shelters can take a variety of forms depending on the situation and context. You should learn how to construct an emergency shelter using the adze of the ice axe alone, as you are unlikely to be carrying a snow shovel just when you need it most. It is extremely important to find the right place for the easy

construction of a successful snow hole. Best is a steep bank of deep snow perhaps on the lee side of a small ridge where a lot of snow has accumulated. It is preferable to dig into a steep wall of snow because as you dig the debris will fall away without needing clearing.

Mark a small doorway in the snow just large enough to get into and begin your excavation using the adze. The secret here is to dig uphill. Once you have gone into the slope a little, start to chop snow from the top of your shelter. This way the blocks of snow you chop out will fall out of your cave and slide away down the slope. Keep digging upwards and inwards until you have just enough room to get yourself inside in a sitting position. Smooth off the walls and ceiling with a gloved hand as this will help prevent dripping should the temperature get above zero. Fashion a seat and insulate it with your rucksack. Outside the snow cave you should leave ski poles or an axe standing up in the snow. You can also string out some rope if you have it. These will make you easier to find should a rescue party come by. Remember that it may snow heavily overnight so the more

A winter mountain leader group excavating snow shelters.

A comfortable Snow-hole, complete with shelf space.

markers indicating your position the better. Inside the shelter try to seal off the doorway, which should be down near your feet, and make a small breather hole. Make yourself as comfortable as possible using any spare clothing and your bivouac bag. You should be able to complete an emergency snow hole such as this in about 15 or 20 minutes.

Planned snow holes can be much larger and more comfortable. A snow shovel and perhaps a snow saw will make the job a lot easier. However, even with these tools it usually takes between one and two hours to complete the task. In addition you are likely to get soaked, both by wet snow and sweat, by the time you are finished. For this reason it may be a good idea to remove some layers of clothing before starting, so that you have some dry clothes to put on when finished. If there are two people working on your shelter, mark out two doorways beside each other. Each person can then dig inwards and upwards into the slope. When each is far enough into the slope simply excavate out between the two tunnels, flatten off the floor and smooth the walls and ceiling to reduce drips. You may then wish to block off one of the entrances with snow blocks and perhaps reduce the size of the remaining doorway to reduce heat loss.

Mixed Climbing

Once you have become proficient at navigation and survival, and honed some basic winter mountain skills, you are ready to start winter climbing on the steeper routes. To climb in snow and ice conditions often requires more foresight than climbing in the mountains in summer. For example, it is often difficult and dangerous to fit crampons only when they become necessary. Far better to have anticipated their requirement and fitted them somewhere beforehand.

One important mountaineering skill is the ability to stay comfortable in inclement conditions. Extensive experience of walking and navigation in the winter mountain environment is essential before starting on the frozen crags. With this experience you will already know how cope in the cold and will be able to comfortably endure an hour or so belaying your partner. Be aware that patience can sometimes run thin when you and your climbing partner are both beginners. Climbing and protecting your first pitches in winter conditions can take a long time. It may not seem long when you are climbing, but may seem like an eternity when you are holding the ropes while watching the weather deteriorate or darkness approaching. On harder mixed climbs it is not uncommon to spend two or three hours on one belay stance, as your partner seconds the pitch below, sorts out the rack and then leads the pitch above.

Try not to make unnecessary movements while you are climbing. Make each action count. Your gear is likely to be more spaced than it would be in summer so it is important to find really good placements. Remember, if you fall off, the gear will have to hold not just you but also your axes, crampons and rucksack. Finding good gear placements on mixed winter routes will take time in the beginning. Every crack will be blocked with snow and ice, and the entire surface of the rock may be hoar-frosted. Only experience will give you an eye for likely gear placements.

PROTECTION

The protection you choose to carry will differ greatly depending on the route you are aiming to climb and the conditions you expect to climb in. Sometimes cams are rendered useless because every crack is lined with ice. In these circumstances the cam just slides out on loading rather than camming into the sides of the crack. It is pointless carrying ice screws on a mixed route unless you know that there will be an

ice pitch. Warthogs can be useful if the best protection is provided by frozen turf.

While the use of pegs (or pitons) is often frowned upon in summer climbing venues, their use in winter is generally acceptable. Pegs can normally be removed again by the second, who will also be carrying a hammer, and the damage they cause

Belaying on the Message. (The Mess of Pottage, Cairngorms)

already been used. To improve the reliability of nut runners placed in winter it is usual to tap them into place with the point of the pick. This prevents an otherwise well-placed runner from lifting out as you progress upwards. Be careful not to damage the wire when tapping a nut in this way. The second climber should be able to tap the nut out again using an axe. For this reason it is unnecessary to carry a nut key in winter. A couple of long slings are worth carrying, not only to save rope in belays but also as runners around rock spikes.

With so much protection to carry, many climbers use a bandoleer rather than the gear loops on the harness alone. Too much gear clipped to your harness tends to pull down over your hips no matter how tight you cinch the waist belt. It can also be easier to access the gear with gloved hands when it is clipped to a bandoleer at chest level. The other advantage of the bandoleer is that it is quickly passed to your partner when it is his or her turn to lead.

MIXED CLIMBING TECHNIQUES

The term 'mixed climbing' really refers to a number of types of winter climb. There may be only snowed-up or hoar-frosted rock, there may be frozen turf, or there may be some snow-ice on the route in conjunction with either rock or turf. Usually mixed climbing refers to the ascent of buttress routes where the climbing is mainly on snowed-up rock and/or turf.

A great way to enhance your confidence and technique in mixed climbing is to find a suitable area to practise bouldering with axes and crampons. Do not practise using your axes and crampons in any established summer rock-climbing venue, or even anywhere where people might go climbing or bouldering in summer. They will not be amused to find your scratch marks on the rocks. Find an unfrequented area with plenty of cracks in the rock and a good soft grassy landing. Wear your helmet, gloves and as much protective clothing as you can, as it is likely you will either fall or jump off. Falling or jumping, from even a couple of feet is a lot more dangerous with crampons and axes. Try to land with your feet apart and arms away from your face. Also make sure that should the axe slip out unexpectedly it cannot hit you in the face.

AXE PLACEMENT

Nothing offers such a feeling of security as a good axe placement in frozen turf. Swing the pick deliberately into good frozen turf and you often get the feeling that even if both feet came off, you would still be held secure on one axe. Sometimes, however, the turf is less secure. Early in the winter season the

Mixed climbing combines a number of different winter climb techniques. (Mega Byte, The Cobbler, Arrochar Alps)

to the rock is arguably of less importance than on summer rock climbs. Pegs are best used only in places where other gear, such as rocks, cannot be used effectively. This is because it takes more time and effort to place and remove a peg. Pegs are also often useful as anchors in belays. In such situations both hands are free to place the peg and often a solid anchor is the result of a well-placed peg. Be sure to learn how to place pegs correctly and remember never to place two pegs together in the same crack, as placing the second peg will most likely loosen the first.

As the harder mixed climbs are often snowed-up rock routes, the quality and frequency of protection needs to be higher on these routes. As you will want to place more gear on a hard winter route, a large amount of protection is required. On such mixed routes it is not uncommon to carry a double set of rocks, simply to ensure you have the right size when you need it. It is hard to beat a good rock placement for security, and it is frustrating not to be able to use one because the particular size needed has of axe placement possible may make this seem less formidable. One of the most secure axe placements in rock is known as a hook. An ideal place for a hook placement is wherever you find a natural choke stone in a crack or chimney. Simply place the axe over the point where the choke stone meets the side of the crack or chimney to provide an extremely secure placement. Remember that because your wrists are supported inside the wrist loops, climbing with axes puts less strain on your forearms than in climbing with your hands. Even the overhanging tops of boulder-choked chimneys can be surmounted without great difficulty as there are usually plenty of good hook placements around the sides of the choked stones.

If no hooks can be found, the next best type of axe placement is the torque. This is where the pick is placed in a narrow crack while the shaft of the axe is gradually pushed or pulled to one side so that the pick 'torques', or twists, firmly into place. Holding the axe at the bottom of the shaft means the leverage on the pick is immense, so you need to be careful not to break the pick. To reduce leverage, hold the axe further up the shaft, or even by the head. Moving up on a torqued axe is also more difficult than on a hooked one. The sideways pressure on the shaft must be continually maintained to keep the axe in place. Therefore, torquing requires good use of the feet and bodyweight to allow

Sometimes it is better to use hand-holds rather than axes. (Pot of Gold)

turf is often not properly frozen under the snow. When unfrozen, climbing on turf can be very dangerous. Whole clods of turf can dislodge as you attempt to pull up, or the axes can rip through, sending you flying. On some very popular mixed routes the turf has gradually disappeared over time. In some cases this has made the routes harder, as the absence of turf requires more rock handholds and axe placements.

Climbing hoar-frosted rock using axes and crampons may seem daunting in the beginning. An understanding of the different types

Back and footing on Stirling Bomber. (Coire an Sneachda)

Coping with the varying conditons found in mixed-climbing will test your skills and ingenuity. (Tilt, Coire an Lochan, Glencoe)

movement upwards without disturbing the axe placement. Other parts of the axe can be torqued in addition to the pick. The hammer can sometimes be torqued, resulting in a more robust placement as more pressure can be applied without fear of breakage. In wider cracks the adze can be torqued into place, and very occasionally the shaft of the axe can be placed in a horizontal crack and twisted to jam it in place. The only limiting factor in the use of the axe will be your own ingenuity, as it can be used any way which will allow upward progress.

OTHER TECHNIQUES

If the route is well snowed-over or the hoar frost on the rock is thick, a good deal of clearing will be necessary. For this it is normal to use the adze, the shaft or your hands and arms – in fact anything which will clear enough snow and ice for you to find the next hold or placement. Therefore, the best conditions for mixed climbing occur when there is enough hoar frost to cover the rocks, but not so much that a lot of time is needed for clearing the route. When a lot of clearing is necessary it can be

A well hoar-frosted mixed route.

easier to follow another party up a route as all the holds will already have been cleared.

Climbing with crampons on steep rock takes some getting used to. Try to place at least two points on each rock hold. Sometimes this requires an unusual angle for the foot but is preferable to using only one point, which can feel wobbly and insecure. Try to keep your boot perfectly still as you move up on the foothold. Any movement of the points on the rock-hold will feel very insecure and may well dislodge it.

Belays in mixed climbing are often similar to those in rock climbing. Rock-based protection, such as spikes, nuts or pegs is likely to be stronger and faster to place (and remove) than turf or ice-based protection. Dig, kick or cut a comfortable flat stance for the belay out of the snow or ice. It is worth the short time this takes for the extra leg room it provides on the belay.

Ice bouldering is extremely good for gaining confidence.

Ice Climbing

The first thing you will learn about ice is that it usually feels much steeper than it really is. To measure the angle of an ice slope, take an axe and position it vertically with the point touching the ice. Take another axe and place this horizontally across the top of the first axe. If it just touches the slope and the handle of the other axe, the angle of slope you are on is around 45°. If it forms a 'T' with the vertical axe, the slope angle is greater than 45°.

All the crampon techniques discussed have two basic principles. The first is to keep as many of the crampon points as firmly in the ice as possible, while the second is to keep the foot stationary in the ice as you take your step over it. For this reason, supple ankles and good balance are essential for good crampon technique. When walking on low-angled ice, keep your feet a little wider apart than normal to avoid snagging crampons. Walking up very low-angled inclines is possible by splaying the feet apart slightly so that your toes are pointing outwards and slightly uphill. This will help you keep your foot flat, and so keep more points in the ice. On low-angled slopes it is easier to hold the axe by the head in the uphill hand using the spike to aid balance.

FOOT PLACEMENT

As the angle increases it becomes necessary to zig-zag upwards. Your feet should be placed across the slope with your toes pointing slightly downhill. The axe may be held with the head in the downhill hand and the shaft held diagonally across your body in the other hand. This allows you to place the spike in the ice to aid balance. The most difficult part of this technique is moving over your uphill foot. On this foot the ankle will be turned outwards with the flat of the foot on the slope. Putting your weight on a foot placed in this way will take some getting used to. It is easier to lean slightly into the slope, using the spike of the axe for balance and bring the trailing foot up while leaning on the axe. You will therefore be alternately in balance and out of balance with each step.

As you step up, make sure you do not let the angle of the sole of your foot change in the slope. This can easily cause the lower, inside of the crampon to lift off the ice, causing the outside edge points to shear out of the ice completely. Move the axe before each step and keep it in place during each step. Do not be tempted to try to save time by moving axe and crampons at the same time.

To change direction when zig-zagging like this, step through as before, but this time place your upper foot with your toes pointing slightly uphill. Then swing your lower foot out in the opposite direction so that you are now splay-footed with your toes pointing in virtually opposite directions across the slope. Because your feet are both sideways in one line across the slope, balance is difficult. Therefore keep the spike of the axe on the ice in front of you on the slope, and keep a little weight leaning in on it. Then simply step over to face your new direction across the slope and place the upper boot, again with sole turned outwards, flat onto the ice. Swap the position of your hands on the axe so that the downhill hand is on the head, and the uphill hand is holding the shaft near the spike.

When the angle of the slope becomes too steep to carry out this splay-footed manoeuvre, it becomes necessary to make an

A spectacular ice formation.

74

The appearance of an ice route can be misleading. It is often steeper than it looks. (Shiva Lingum, Argentière ice falls, France)

intermediate front point placement with the crampon of each foot. Remember only to move one point of contact at a time and make each movement steady and deliberate.

Descending ice slopes of up to 45° is possible facing outwards, although this can feel rather insecure in the beginning. It is necessary to use a general mountaineering axe for this purpose, as a technical axe will not give the security required when placed head downwards in the slope. Face out, toes pointing straight down the slope, and bend your knees so as to plant the axe as low as possible. A slight outward pull on the shaft of the axe will lock it in place and allow you to step down and place a crampon securely on the slope below. It will seem difficult at first to securely plant the sole of your foot on the slope below you. Transfer your weight onto the lower foot and bring the trailing foot down to place it beside the first. Your hand can be moved down the shaft of the ice axe like a hand rail, so it may be possible to take two small steps for each placement of the axe. To release the axe, push the shaft in against the slope, and, holding the head of the axe, pull it out along the smooth upper side of the pick.

On steeper slopes, descent can be made by diagonal zig-zag in the same manner as described above. Whether it is possible to descend facing out depends not only on how steep and how hard the ice slope is, but also on the skill and confidence of the climber.

On steeper inclines of over 45° it becomes too difficult to keep the flat of both feet on the ice, there being a limit to the suppleness of even the best climber's ankles. Therefore, once a certain slope angle has been reached, it becomes necessary to use the front points of one or both crampons. Using the front points of one crampon, while the other is turned out to one side

Successful ice-climbing requires a good deal of stamina and expertise.
(Cascade Difficult, Trient, Switzerland)

is a fast and energy-efficient method of ascent. As the calf muscles of one leg tire, simply swap sides and front point with the other foot.

USING THE AXE
The axe can be used in a dagger technique by holding the head of the axe around the adze and placing the pick into the ice. The shaft of the axe lies down along the surface of the slope when using this technique. This technique is useful on slope angles not steep enough to warrant holding the shaft, as it is quick to place and remove. In addition, more steps can be taken per axe placement, because it is possible to move quite high in relation to

the axe. The climber may be in a mantle position on the head of the axe before it is necessary to remove it.

As the angle gets steeper it becomes necessary to hold the axe by the bottom of the shaft. This allows it to be swung into the slope rather than stabbed. When you are learning to swing an axe, try to do so in a smooth, controlled fashion. In particular, learn to swing the axe keeping the pick perfectly straight in the line of the swing. Any deviation between the angle of the pick and the angle of the swing and you will not get the best placement possible. Once placed it is often useful to place your other hand over the head of the axe so that both hands can aid in stability and balance.

Obviously, when using one axe on steep ice you must have good faith in your front point placements, because it is necessary to remove the axe in order to place it higher. Make sure that your points bite into the ice, not by kicking hard, but rather by keeping your heel low as you place the front points. If you notice your toe bounce off the ice when you attempt to kick the front points in, this is probably because the heel is too high. When the heel is too high, the upper toe of the boot meets the ice, rather than the front points. The need to keep the heel low when kicking-in can make the descent of steep ice difficult. This is because of the need to place the front points below you with a straight leg while keeping the heel low and the toe up. Supple hamstrings are obviously an advantage.

On very steep ice it becomes impossible to balance on your front points alone. The use of two technical axes is therefore necessary. Remember to place your second ice tool far enough apart from the first so as not to affect the strength of the ice around the first placement. Do not make the mistake of placing your ice tools too high while climbing steep ice, as this will make it difficult to see what you doing with your feet. In addition, if a tool is not placed properly, and you need to get it out to place it again, this will be very difficult if you have also placed it at arm's length above your head. Try not to overgrip the shafts of the axes until your forearms are burning. Rather, relax a little and let the wrist loops take the strain. Neither should you hold onto the axes with bent arms for long periods, as this will require too much strength. Rather, hang out a bit from the ice on straight arms, which will be much less strenuous.

Make sure that each time you place the axe it is a solid placement. Remember that you are going to remove the other axe and so will rely totally on each axe placement. In many conditions it pays to pick the spot where you make your

Difficulty is relative to experience. (Cogne, Italy.)

placements. For example, patches of whiter snow ice among harder, clearer ice can make for really solid axe placements, and even the smallest ripples or bumps on water ice can make front point placements much more secure.

Clearing the top of a steep ice pitch can be a moment of great relief, although great care is required. The temptation is to lean forwards over the easier angled slope above steep ice. This can cause the heels to raise and the front points to jump out of their placements. For this reason you should keep the axe placements low and walk the front points up over the steep ice before standing upright.

PROTECTION

Protection on ice usually takes the form of ice screws and snargs. Clear away any loose ice or debris on the surface to expose good quality ice before beginning. If the ice around the screw shatters while it is being placed, this too must be cleared away until the screw is placed in good quality ice. It may be necessary to angle the screw slightly down into the ice for the

best placement, although this depends on the ice quality. Be sure never to place an axe too close to an ice screw, as this will weaken the ice around the protection.

Some ice screws do not have slots to allow jammed ice to be cleared, and in many conditions such screws can only be used once. Therefore try to get screws with slots. Titanium screws are much lighter than steel but some varieties are made from very soft metal which will be ruined by contact with the rock if ice screws do not penetrate the ice fully so always tie them off, using an inverted clove hitch on a sling.

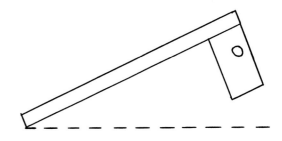

Ice screw angle approximately 100°.

ICE CLIMBING

Mixed climbing, (The Crack, Northern Corries, Scotland.)

Overseer Direct, Coire Lochan, Scotland.

When belaying on ice, first cut a ledge out of the slope at least wide enough to stand on. Place a good screw high on one side and clove hitch into it. Place a screw on the other side and clove hitch into it with the other rope. You may also back up these anchors by placing your axes high in the middle and clipping into these with a sling. If desired, another krab can be clipped to the first screw and the climbing rope clipped through it as a runner. This screw will in any case form the first runner when your partner leads off on the next pitch.

Often natural protection, such as ice pillars, can be found on ice routes. These simply require a sling passed around them. Occasionally thread belays can be fashioned by making two holes though a hollow section of ice and passing a sling through one and out of the other. Such protection, in good ice conditions, can be very strong indeed.

Be aware that the quality of ice varies widely from rotten water ice through to perfect white snow ice, so don't be put off if your first experiences of steep ice climbing were unpleasant. It may just have been the ice.

Winter Climbing Grades: A Comparison

INTRODUCTION

With winter climbing that is anything involving climbing ice, snow, rock, turf or any combination thereof, there has been a general rise in standards over all countries This, coupled with increased specialisation and development of new styles (e.g. dry tooling) has led to a gradual evolution of new grading systems.

Most of the systems used may on first glance appear the same but different regions usually use very different systems. This chapter contains a brief outline of the thinking behind the main grading systems and how they are used, together with a comparison of several routes, showing the main differences.

It should be borne in mind that within any grading system used in winter climbing, the actual grade of a given route can vary enormously. Good ice, poor ice, thin ice, no ice, heavy snow cover or no snow cover can all affect the grade of a route from season to season, and even day to day. When a grade is given for a route it is usually for the average condition of the route.

SCOTLAND

Introduced in 1991, this is a two-tier system in which Roman numerals denote the overall difficulty of the climb, while an Arabic numeral indicates the technical difficulty of the hardest sections. Nearly all climbs up to grade IV retain a straightforward overall grade (I–IV), although some grade III climbs do have a technical grade. Point Five gully on Ben Nevis is seen as the benchmark Scottish V 5 ice route. The V indicates reasonably sustained climbing, but with gear perhaps being difficult to arrange. A technical grade of 5 indicates relatively straightforward steep ice climbing. What makes the Scottish system unique is that it is designed to cover an enormous range of climbing styles and mediums.

CANADA

The Canadian system was developed to mainly cover water ice routes. Like the Scots, the Canadian system is two-tiered. It also

Summit ridge, Mt. Sir Douglas, Canadian Rockies, East Ridge.

includes acommitment grade (using Roman numerals I–VII) with each grade having a unique description detailing the approach, length of route, objective dangers etc. This is coupled with a technicalgrade (Degree 1–8) which grades the actual climbing. Again, each technical grade has a specific description e.g. a Canadian 3 has sustained ice up to 80 degrees, and requires technique to arrange adequate protection and belays. It may also have short sections of steeper ice, usually with good rest in-between. The quality of the ice will generally be good. For climbs that are seriously thin and run out, a Seriousness grade using R (for runout) and or X (for fragile climbs prone to collapse) is added. If we take our benchmark Scottish route Point Five gully, it's grade using the Canadian system would be IV 4. The US system is broadly similar, but has different classifications such as Alpine ice and Water ice.

THE EUROPEAN CONTINENT

The French system for steep ice is almost identical to that used in Canada. So popular has this system become it has started to be used for grading Alpine ice routes, sometimes in preference to the old UIAA Alpine grades. The French system is

A comparison of grading systems is useful when visiting a new area.

now in widespread use throughout Europe. Again it is a two tier system with a commitment grade (Grade D'engagement) of I–VII, and a technical grade (Degré technique) of 1–7. So that a Point Five gully would roughly equate to a IV 4 in Europe.

CONCLUSIONS

Regions have evolved grading systems to generally reflect the type of winter climbing commonplace on their home ground. All the grading systems outlined above are fully described in the appropriate guidebooks, and once you have used them a few times, they will be easy to understand. However, it is important to fully understand the differences. A Scottish V 6 would usually be a reasonably protected Scottish mixed type route, perhaps on snowed up rock. On the other hand a French V 6 would usually mean a big face exposed to weather and avalanche risk, with a difficult approach (glaciated) and descent. The 6 would indicate vertical to overhanging technical ice, with protection being difficult to arrange or non-existent.

New wave mixed climbing: hard rock in the ice. (Cogne, Italy)

Climbing
Around
The World

INTRODUCTION

This section takes a look at the wide variety of climbing venues that can be found around the world. It is intended as an guide to some of the most popular or best-established climbing areas worldwide, and includes both ice and rock climbing regions. The potential for adventure climbing around the world, in remote and rarely travelled areas remains unlimited, and to all intents and purposes it always will.

This introductory guide extends from rock climbing on the crags of Europe to the big walls of Yosemite in the US and Norway. Mountaineering venues covered include Nepal's misnamed

'trekking peaks', European venues such the Alps, New Zealand, Greenland and South America. Pure ice climbing can be found in Canada and in the French Alps. Several excellent rock climbing venues are covered, and these include the Scottish Highlands and Snowdonia in the UK, and the Eldorado Canyon in the US.

Information on each region includes issues such as the best climbing season and the weather to climb, local climbing ethics and traditions and any particular skills required for successful climbing or mountaineering in the area. Special considerations and points to remember are also noted.

The Alps

Forming an impressive natural boundary between France, Switzerland, Austria, Slovenia and Italy, the European Alps are probably the most climbed mountains in the world. Their popularity is entirely warranted. First climbed in 1786, Mont Blanc has a unique place in mountaineering history and attracts thousands of suitors throughout the year. But it is just one of thousands of mountains in this massive chain. On these great peaks some of the world's finest mountaineers have honed their skills on snow, ice and rock before taking up the challenge of the world's untouched summits. Climbing all 61 independent summits of 4000m (13123 feet) and above is a project of a lifetime for many others, requiring the ability to move safety and fast over snow, ice, rock of all descriptions and frequently heavily crevassed glacial terrain.

Looking from the Valtournanche area of the Italian Alps to the Dent Blanche, the pyramid on the left, the Dent d'Herens, centre , the Matterhorn.

It is and indication of the quality of climbs in the Alps that the great six pre-war North Faces of the Matterhorn, Petit Dru, Grandes Jorasses, Piz Badile, Eiger and the Cima Grande continue to attract today's climbers. An assent of the Walker Spur on the Grandes Jorasses is the zenith of many mountaineer's achievements.

Alongside these are thousands of other routes; long and committing climbs up massive mixed faces and pinnacled ridges, plus many more amenable routes. For those who remain uninspired by the impressive spires of ice-bound granite surrounding the town of Chamonix-Mt Blanc, there are the dramatic snowy mountains of Switzerland's Pennine Alps and Bernese Oberland, or the quieter, but no less impressive, regions of the Ecrins and Bernina.

At lower altitudes rock abounds, principally quality faces of granite and limestone and in recent years these have become gradually more developed, as have the paths and long distance trails which make back – packing a delight throughout the alpine chain.

Mt. Blanc from the Val Ferret in Italy.

FACT FILE

Seasons: January to March and June to September. Climate warming means the big ice faces are safest early and late in the season. Bad weather and objective dangers, most recently from climate warming, are always present in the high mountains.

Prominent peaks: Mont Blanc (4807m/15771ft), Matterhorn (4477m/14688 ft), Grandes Jorasses (4208m/13806 ft), Eiger (3970m/13025 ft).

Bases: Chamonix (Fr), Courmayeur (It), Aosta (It), Zermatt (Sw), Grindelwald (Sw), Vicosoprano (Sw), Innsbruck (Aus).

Activities: Mountaineering, traditional and bolt protected rock-climbing, ice climbing, skiing and back packing. In all countries, hundreds of rock-climbing areas lie within a short drive of the mountains.

Special considerations: Good food, good wine, good campsites, transport, mountain access and rescue services.

Guidebooks: *The Alpine 4000m Peaks* by Richard Goedeke (Diadem), *The High Mountains of the Alps* (Baton Wicks/The Mountaineers). The European Alpine Clubs all publish a number of guidebooks in their respective languages.

The north face of the Grandes Jorasses, Chamonix, French Alps. The Walker Spur is the buttress on the left.

France

The two most popular areas are Oisans and the six valleys, Argentière La Bessée Chamonix and Briancon. Guidebooks are available for both these areas and are easily purchased at local climbing shops.

WEATHER

The season tends to last from early December to early March. Ideal conditions tend to be when high pressure predominates. Clear days and temperature inversions tend to produce good climbing conditions. However, bad weather, particularly if it arrives from the south, can produce extremely hazardous conditions with heavy snowfall and a correspondingly high increase in the avalanche risk.

ACCESS

Public transport is not the best in the area. To maximise the amount of ice climbed you really need your own transport. Hire cars are expensive in France, so it may pay to drive out there. Snow chains are often obligatory. However, if you prefer to fly

and hire a car, there are regular flights to Geneva, Lyon and Milan, all of which are around a few hours drive to the Ecrins.

VENUES

Alp D'Huez is one of the most accessible venues in the area. It has a superb selection of easy to middle grade routes, the best of which are situated in the ski area. You can use the uplift facilities to the first station where it is a short (15 minutes or so) walk around to the climbs. Most of the routes are relatively short with one or two pitches, and are generally equipped with bolt belays.

One of the best routes in this section is Symphonie D'Automne (120m/394 ft). This is a classic climb, combining a sunny outlook, plentiful ice and contrasting pitches. For an easier climb, then Ice Bille (50m/165 ft) just along the cliff is ideal. Alp D'Huez is a useful venue in that routes are reliable because of their altitude, so you can always be assured of finding some ice to climb.

LA GRAVE AREA

Further down the road towards the Col De Lautaret are several areas containing an impressive number of icefalls. There is a superb variety of routes from modern test pieces to straight-forward steep ice. One of the first routes is called Phantasme, which is a classic 200m (656 ft) route, with limited objective danger and lots of steep ice.

If you prefer a longer route, then drive to Caturgeas. After completing the climb it is possible to walk over to the ski area at Chazalet, although ensure you have a map and compass if it is misty.

VALLON DU DIABLE

This area has an excellent selection of classic ice routes, generally in the middle to upper end of the grading scale, although there is increased avalanche risk. Most of the routes are on the north side of the valley, but there are few quality routes that face south. If you are climbing south-facing routes, watch out for falling ice and avalanche activity when the sun hits the upper slopes.

Vol Du Bourdon (280m/919 ft) is a superb route on plentiful blue ice, fixed belay stations and a sunny aspect. Just across the valley

Crag shot, Argentière La Bessé ice falls..

Mer de Glace, Chamonix.

FACT FILE
When to visit: Early December to early March.

Popular climbs: Symphonie D'Automne, Ice Bille in Alp D'Huez, Phantasme, Caturgeas in La Grave, Vol Du Bourdon, Les Hemos A Godo, Cristal Palace in Vallon du Diable, Palais des Glaces in Fournel, Tete de Gramusat in Freissinieres.

Access: Regular flights to Geneva, Lyon and Milan. Cars can reach most routes, although in heavy snow snow chains may be necessary. Skis or snowshoes may be necessary.

Activities: All types of ice climbing from easy to extreme.

Special considerations: To minimise avalanche and ice fall danger, it is recommended that you start and finish your climbs early.

from this is Les Hemos A Godo (220m/722 ft). This route is exposed to avalanche and/or spindrift when there is a lot of snow about. For extreme ice climbing, try Cristal Palace. This has limited protection and steep to overhanging ice combined with technical and athletic climbing.

FOURNEL
The Fournel Valley is situated just outside Argentière La Bessée, near Briancon. Conditions are usually reliable and you have a choice of over 80 routes both south and north facing. Davidoff is the most accessible sector, as well as the most filmed. However, the most beautiful climb is arguably the Palais des Glaces, which has a superb variety of steep ice falls. The best route here is Delicados(250m/820 ft).

FREISSINIERES
Situated near Argentière La Bessèe is the Freissinieres Valley. Most routes are concentrated either on the Tete de Gramusat or just across from it on some steep cliffs. The routes here are easily accessible and fairly short, although they do provide good sport. However, the north face of the Tete de Gramusat has a superb selection of extreme ice routes, all around 300m+ (984 ft+) and all very serious.

Argentière Ice Falls.

Spain

The past decade has transformed rock-climbing in Spain from an interesting alternative to a week on the beach with the family, to one of the premier locations for European sport-climbers. The Pyrenees and the limestone mountains of the Picos de Europa on Spain's Atlantic Coast have always attracted climbers and mountain walkers, especially the impressive 500m (1640 ft) face of Naranjo de Bulnes.

Further east, in the foothills of the Pyrenees are the amazing red conglomerate spires of Los Mallos above the small village of Riglos. These 300m (984 ft) bolt-protected faces offer climbing

on bizarre rock and are very much an acquired taste. A good introduction to this area are the smaller conglomerate spires round the monastery of Montserrat west of Barcelona.

Moving down the Mediterranean coast to Valencia are the limestone areas of Montanejos with its thermal springs and Chulilla with its Moorish castle. South again, the resorts of Calpe, Benidorm and Alicante offer the largest concentration of rock-climbing in Spain. Once heat and holiday makers have dispersed, this area becomes a Mecca for climbers, encouraged by excellent facilities and off-season rates. There are many superb areas both on the coast and inland, but for those of an

Un Dia de Playa, El Corral, El Chorro.

Los Muyayos, El Corral, El Chorro.

exploratory bent the mountain cliffs of Puig Divino and Puig Campana outside Benidorm offer an opportunity to escape from too many climbers. Further south in Andalusia and close to the resort of Malaga lies the limestone gorge of El Chorro and the Sierra Nevada mountains. Mulhacen is the highest mountain in Spain and withits neighbours, Alcazaba and Veleta it offers a variety of mountain and ice climbs, mainly in the winter months.

Finally, the rugged limestone mountains of Mallorca's north-west coast give challenging mountain walks and scrambles. Again, popular with climbers off-season, more and more of the cliffs are being developed.

Limestone cliffs on the Fermentor peninsular, on the north-west tip of Mallorca.

FACT FILE

When to Visit: The Pyrenees and Picos de Europa are better in summer. Most of the other areas come into their own during autumn, winter and spring. The Sierra Nevada are best in winter and spring.

Prominent peaks: Naranjo de Bulnes (2519m/8264 ft), Mulhacen (3482m/11424 ft) Alcazaba (3363m/11034 ft) Veleta (3398m/11148 ft).

Bases: Oviedo, Valencia, Alicante, Calpe, Benidorm, Malaga, Palma.

Activities: Mostly bolt protected rock-climbing, mountain walking and scrambling. Longer traditionally protected routes do exist, mostly on the larger mountain faces.

Special considerations: Good food, good wine, good campsites, transport, mountain access and health services.

Guidebooks: *Costa Blanca Rock* by Chris Craggs, *Costa Blanca* by Alan James, *Climbing in Spain* by Francois Burnier and Dominique Potard, *Picos de Europa* by Robin Walker. Numerous guidebooks exist in all languages.

Italy

Although Italy shares its frontier with many of the great high peaks in the alps, Mt Blanc, the Matterhorn and Pizzo Bernina, only a few ranges lie wholly within its borders. North-west of Turin, the Gran Paradiso area contains one of the more straight-forward 4000m (13123 feet) peaks and the spectacular granite faces of the Valle dell'Orco. It is easily accessed from Chamonix through the Mt Blanc tunnel.

On the east side of the alpine chain, south of the Austrian border are the awe-inspiring limestone towers and faces of the Dolomites. After more than 60 years Riccado Cassin and Emilio Comici's respective routes on the north faces of the Cima Ovest

Extreme ice, Candeloni Di Patri, Cogne.

Far Right: Sass Pordoi, south pillar, Dolomites.

Marmolada, highest peak in the Dolomites, sunset on the immense south face.

pocketed limestone. Throughout Italy, more limestone cliffs are developed every year, one of the most recent areas being the Mediterranean island of Sardinia. Finally, the Apennine Mountains run the full length of Italy. The highest peaks of the Grand Sasso area, the Corno Grande and Corno Piccolo lie east of Rome and offer both winter mountaineering and summer rock-climbing. Extreme ice climbing can be found at Cogne.

and Cima Grande are free climbing experiences high on the hit-lists of many climbers.

The highest peak in the Dolomites is the Marmolata. In recent years, developments on its 700m south face have established an array of impressive highly technical multi-day limestone climbs.

The best known of these is probably the Fish Route; a stunning 25+ pitch bolt-free experience of great technicality. Classic mountain rock-climbs offer easier ways to the summits as do a profusion of Via Ferrata; prepared ways utilising fixed cables, ladders and natural terraces up the great peaks and faces.

On the many limestone cliffs developed outside of the mountains, one of the most popular is Finale Ligure, along the coast from Monaco on the Gulf of Genoa. Here a range of bolt protected routes at all grades can be found on cliffs of perfect

---

FACT FILE

When to Visit: Summer and winter for the mountains. Out of the mountains late spring and early autumn are probably best for all but lizards.

Prominent peaks: Monte Bianco (4807m/15771 ft),
Monte Cervino/Matterhorn (4477m/14688ft),
Pizzo Bernina(4049m/13284 ft),
Gran Paradiso (4061m/13323 ft),
Marmolata (3344m/10971ft),
Cima Grande (2999m/9839 ft),
Cima Ovest (2973m/9754 ft),
Corno Grande (2912m/9554ft),
Corno Piccolo (2655m/8711 ft).

Bases: Aosta, Como, Bolzano, Finale Ligure.

Activities: All styles of climbing and mountain walking are catered for.

Special considerations: Good food, good wine, good campsites, transport, mountain access and health services.

Guidebooks: *Central Apennines of Italy* by Stephen Fox, *Italian Rock* by Al Churcher, *Via Ferrata* by Hofler Werner. Numerous local guidebooks exist.

United Kingdom

SCOTLAND

Scotland contains the highest, steepest and most remote cliffs of the UK, and has possibly the most varied and complex geology of any country of comparable size. It is this rich variety of rock types, together with a diverse range of venues, which makes Scotland such a memorable place to climb.

On the mainland, the north face of Britain's highest peak Ben Nevis has a number of climbs of almost alpine stature, including the aptly named Long Climb. The neighbouring Glen Coe contains the most accessible mountains. One of the most varied mountains is the distinctive triangular-shaped Buachaille Etive Mor, overlooking the barren Rannock Moor. Routes range

Psychedelic Wall, Ben Nevis, Scotland.

from the straightforward Curved Ridge to the fierce extremes of Creag a'Bhancair. Here on the steep Tunnel Wall are the only mountain sports climbs in the UK.

For remote climbing, try Carn Mor, found deep within the Letterewe and Fisherfield Forest, an area commonly known as 'the last great wilderness'. Similarly remote are the corries found in the Cairngorms, such as Coire Sputan Dearg and Creag a Choire Etchachan. The easiest approach to these is from Braemar on Royal Deeside. This area contains Britain's second highest mountain – Ben Macdui.

As well as mountain-climbing, the Highlands of Scotland are also famed for their low-lying climbing venues. These include Glen Nevis, Craig-a-Barns and Creag Dhubh in the Central Highlands. Further north and west new crags such as Stone Valley and Creagan Dubha have been developed, while further north still, Seanna Mheallan and Ardmair are perfect for brushing up on technique.

The islands of Scotland also contain much of interest, ranging from the highest of the Orkney Isles, which features both the Old Man of Hoy, a towering stack of sandstone standing 130m (427 ft) above the sea, and St. John's Head, the highest sea cliff in Britain at 400m (1312 ft). The Isle of Lewis contains some of the finest and oldest rock in the world, while its neighbour, Harris, contains the steepest cliff in Britain – Sron Ulladale. Two new venues can be found on the tiny islands of Mingulay and Pabbay, at the extreme southern end of the Western Isles. Reached by fishing boat from Barra, these islands have two fine cliffs. While the Great Arch on Pabbay has repulsed all attempts so far, Dun Mingulay has around a dozen quality routes.

ENGLAND

Peak District

Regarded by many devotees as the epicentre of British climbing, the Peak District is ideal for both sports climbing and bouldering. Close to Sheffield lie the famed Gritstone edges, where a strict no piton, bolt-free ethic make for some of the boldest climbs anywhere. Ravens Tor harbours many of the hardest routes, including one of the world's hardest – Hubble. Some fine bouldering can be found, often around the base of the edges themselves.

The Flying Dutchman, Glen Nevis, Scotland

Climbing on the impressive granite cliff at Bosigran, on the toe of Cornwall.

Lake District

Celebrated as the birthplace of British rock climbing, with a diverse range of volcanic venues, such as Borrowdale and Langdale. Some of the biggest and best cliffs include Dow Crag, Esk Buttress and the most famous Scafell Crag. Sport routes can be found within the remnant slate quarries, as well as at Chapel Head Scar and St. Bees Head.

The South West

Cornwall presents a diverse range of coastal crags within West Penwith, England's most south-westerly peninsula. The sea-cliffs vary from the fine granite crags around Land's End, of which Bosigran is probably the most popular, through to the dark and foreboding shale cliffs on the north coast. Other fine venues include Sennen, Chair Ladder, Carn Barra and Lundy Island, with fine granite cliffs up to 100 m (328 ft).

Yorkshire

The three main climbs of this region are found on the limestone crags of Malham Cove, Gordale Scar and Kilnsey Crag, although smaller climbs can also be found at Ilkley, Caley Crags and Almscliff.

WALES

Pembroke

Among the most atmospheric of the limestone crags of the South Pembrokeshire coast is Huntsman Leap, a chasm running perpendicular to the coast, which narrows to just a few metres at its seaward end. The Crystal Slabs and Mosaic Wall of Flimston Bay provide the best low-angled routes on the coast.

North Wales

Running through the heart of Snowdonia, the Llanberis Pass is lined with many of the best crags, including Dinas Cromlech, Dinas Mot and Cwym Glas Bach. In the neighbouring Ogwen Valley, the Idwal Slabs make for fine introductory climbing, including the classics Faith, Hope and Charity. For more advanced climbers, the slopes of Snowdon hold Clogwyn Du'r Arddu and the serious Indian Face. Gogarth, on the island of

Milky Way, Ilkley Crag, Yorkshire.

Anglesey contains the most extensively developed sea-cliffs in the country, while sports climbs can be found adjacent to Llandudno on the Ormes, two limestone promontories. One of the best crags is the tidal Lower Pen Trwyn, while the watery approach to the superb Diamond will suit the more adventurous.

FACT FILE

When to visit: Climbing is possible all year round, although excessive snowfall during winter months of November to March can make conditions extremely hazardous in remote areas.

Popular Climbs: Scotland – Ben Nevis, Gen Coe, Carn Mor, Cairngorms, Glen Nevis, Highlands, Lewis and Harris Islands. England – Gritstone Edges, Raven's Tor in the Peak District, Scafell Crag in the Lake District, Lands End in Cornwall. Wales Huntsman Leap, South Pembroke, Snowdonia.

Access: Most climbs in the UK are easily accessible by road and foot. For more remote areas provision should be made for long walks, while some islands will require specially chartered boats for access.

Activities: The UK contains a rich diversity of ice and rock climbing, bouldering and sports climbs. Special Considerations: if climbing in remote areas prone to adverse weather conditions, such as parts of Scotland, Wales and the Peak District, always check local advance weather reports before setting out.

Gragarth, Anglesey, N. Wales.

The Direct Route, Dinas Mot, Llanberis Pass, Wales.

Norway

Although much of the high land is snow-covered in winter, Norway has a few areas of permanent glacier in summer. North-west of Oslo is the Jostedalsbreen and the Jotunheimen. The former is the largest ice-field in Europe, the latter contains Galdhopiggen, Norway's highest mountain, which with Glittertind nearby, give straightforward snow ascents.

To the north, just inland from the coast at Andalsnes is the Romsdal valley. Over the years its massive walls have fallen in and out of favour with climbers and in 1998 the impressive Troll Wall suffered a massive rock fall, reflecting the inherent structural instability of big walls. The 1,370m (4495 feet) Troll Wall lies above the main road and is one of tallest pieces of rock in Europe. Recent activity has been on modern technical multi-pitch rock-climbs on smaller road-side buttresses.

Further north above the Arctic Circle the climbing areas offer the unusual experience of a 24 hour daylight summer. From Bodo towards Tysfjord, Narvik and the Lofoten Islands the glaciated granite landscape reveals peaks and soaring granite cliffs at every turn. Two impressive peaks in this area are Eidetind and the flat topped obelisk of Stetind. The latter's huge north-west face offers a 54 pitch rock-climb from fjord to summit. The Lofoten Islands have also become popular

Below the south pillar of Stetind, near Narvik.

Looking across to the impressive granite peak of Eidetind, near Narvik.

recently, mostly the granite faces surrounding the coast, rather than the pinnacles and ridges of the islands' mountains.

Hundreds of miles of tunnel, causeway and ferry make travelling up Norway's west coast a time consuming business, so for those with less time on their hands, the deep glaciated valleys east of Bergen and north-west of Oslo contain many popular cliffs. Among the best of these is Uskeladen, which offers climbs of six to 18 pitches on quality granite. It lies on the edge of the Hardangerfjord, just south of Bergen.

In winter there is a considerable amount of ice climbing on easily accessible frozen waterfalls. However, the development of similar areas in France and Canada makes Norway less popular for visitors.

The impressive north face of Stetind, near Narvik.

FACT FILE

When to visit: June, July, August. Norway's summer weather is similar to Scotland, but more predictable. Heavy winter snowfall means some big north facing walls take time to come into condition. In winter, Febuary, March and April are best for ice-falls.

Prominent peaks: Galdhopiggen (2469m/8100 ft), Glittertind (2452m/8045 ft), Stetind (1392m/4567 ft), Eidetind (846m/2776 ft).

Bases: Oslo, Bergen, Andalsnes, Henninggsvaer, Narvik, Tromso.

Activities: Some mountaineering, but mostly multi-pitch rock-climbs on perfect rock in solitary locations. The ice climbing is excellent.

Special considerations: Expensive, especially for alcohol. Further north the mosquitos, midges and hornets are unbearable. It can drizzle for weeks.

Guidebooks: *Romsdal* by Tony Howard, *Climbing in the Magic Islands (Lofoten)* by Ed Webster. Various guidebooks available locally.

Nepal

The kingdom of Nepal is justly famous as the home of the world's highest mountain – Sagarmatha, otherwise known as Mount Everest. Many other famous peaks can also be found within Nepal, such as Annapurna, Makalu, and Ama Dablam to name just a few. On these larger peaks you would generally need to be part of a special expedition, which may be prohibitive to the ordinary climber due to the cost involved, and the level of climbing skill required. However, you do not have to be a climbing superstar, or extremely rich to climb in the Nepal Himalayas. The deceptively named 'trekking peaks' are a set of 18 mountains ranging between 5587m (18,330ft) and 6654m (21,830ft) in height, and these are free from many of the costs and restrictions of the larger expedition peaks. These peaks offer the opportunity for a group of like-minded friends to organise their own Himalayan expedition within a time scale that most people could manage.

Moreover, Nepal is a wonderful country to visit. Some say that if you drop your camera in Nepal, and the shutter goes off, you will still have a beautiful photograph. It is certainly true that everywhere you look, a stunning view lies before you. The people too are extremely friendly and welcoming.

The main climbing seasons in Nepal are the pre- and post monsoon seasons. These are the spring period (February and March) and the autumn period (October and November) which are the main climbing and trekking high seasons. However, it is very often possible to climb on the trekking peaks right through from October to May, as the weather is generally clear, still and cold in the mid-winter season. The monsoon period lasts from June to September and during this time you can expect rain almost everyday. Leeches are also a very common feature on treks during the monsoon.

There are currently 18 'trekking' peaks, divided into two groups. Cost of permits varies according to which group the peak falls into. Within the more expensive group, highest peaks include Mera Peak in Khumu Himal, Mt. Everest at 6654m (21,831 ft), Chulu East in Manang District, Gandaki at 6584m (21,601 ft) and Singu Chuli (Fluted Peak) in Annapurna Himal, Gandaki at 6501m (21,329 ft). Within the cheaper group, highest peaks are Paldor Peak in Langtang Himal, Bagmati at 5896m (19,344 ft) and Khongma Tse (Mehra Peak) in Khumbu Himal, Mt. Everest at 5849m (19,190 ft).

Kusum Kangru from the trek between Lukla and Namche Bazaar.

Fine views of Ama Dablam from Lobuche SE Ridge.

As well as permit costs, you will also be expected to pay both a National Park fee and a Conservation fee. Fully inclusive tours can be arranged, including everything from porters to carry equipment to catering, or you can arrange everything yourself, including equipment and staff.

The overall seriousness of the trekking peaks varies greatly from peak to peak. Island, Mera and Pisang for instance are generally regarded as fairly straightforward climbs. Kusum Kanguru however is without doubt a committing and difficult objective even by the easiest line of ascent.

To climb in Nepal you must be aware of the dangers of altitude and be able to recognise the early symptoms of Acute Mountain Sickness (AMS). The ability to negotiate glaciers would also be vital for many of the peaks, however, there are also plenty of peaks on which glaciers could be avoided. A high level of cardio-vascular fitness is a distinct advantage for climbing at Nepal's lofty altitudes, and good all round mountaineering skills a necessity to do so safely.

The Far East Summit of Lobuche Peak.

Looking North towards Tibet from the summit of Yala peak. Morimoto is the peak centre-right in the picture.

The beautiful Langtang Valley.

FACT FILE

When to visit: Best end of September through to March.

Access : Fly to Kathmandu, then hike, bus or fly by STOL aircraft and hike to your chosen base camp. There are no roads in the mountains. Highest Trekking Peak – 6654m (21,831 ft).

Activities: Lightweight Alpine climbing trips of one to five days. Mainly snow-ice climbing, snow ridges etc. Experience of glaciers a must on some peaks. Climbs according to difficulty: Kusum Kangru is technically difficult and requires commitment and experience. Pokalde North Ridge and Lobuche South East Ridge, can be climbed in a day or with a high camp at around 5500m (21,831 ft). Most parties go to the false summit or Far East summit.

Special considerations: Views are excellent throughout Nepal, especially the summits of Kongma Tse and Pokalde which overlook the picturesque Ama Dablam, Pumori and the South Face of Nuptse. Also Yala peak in the Langtang valley for views of Langtang Lirung, the beautiful Gangchempo and Naya Kanga.

Australia

Considering most of Australia is uninhabited, it's hardly surprising that the best developed crags lie in the populated south-east of the country, around the principal cities of Adelaide, Melbourne and Sydney and north to Brisbane.

The imposing orange quartzite crags of Mount Arapiles rise straight from the Wimmera Plains in Victoria state, about 300km (186 miles) north-west of Melbourne, midway between that city and Adelaide. Australia's best known climbing area has the highest concentration of hard routes in the country. Up to 100m (328 feet) in places and several kilometres/miles long, there are many different buttresses and faces, each with a unique character and atmosphere.

Moving further west towards Adelaide and South Australia is the magnificent quartzite escarpment of Moonarie. In general the crags are more continuous than at Arapiles and there are many multi-pitch routes. Pride of place goes to the

The Bluffs, Mount Arapiles.

impressively blank looking Great Wall, although there are many middle and easier grade routes. Moonarie lies about 450km (280 miles) north of Adelaide, but closer to the city several small crags of quality quartzite have been developed at Morialta Gorge and Norton Summit.

The imposing Three Sisters in the Blue Mountains.

98

Closer to Melbourne are the quartzite and sandstone crags of the Grampians hills and Mt Buffalo. The reasonable altitude of the latter's granite tors make them a popular venue for local climbers celebrating New Year in the height of summer.

North-east of Melbourne the Snowy Mountains in New South Wales rise to 2,230m (7316 feet) and are popular in summer and winter. Some rock-climbing has been developed. The best area however is at Booroomba Rocks near Canberra in the Australian Capital Territory, which offers good climbing on granite. Further north and back into New South Wales are the

Blue Mountains a few hours drive west of Sydney. This area has been popular with climbers since the 1930s and offers much climbing. The crags form the rim of an extensive sandstone plateau above the plains. Kilometres of rock exist, but impenetrable rain forest makes much of it inaccessible. Mount Piddington is the traditional climbing area with many easy and medium routes. Other areas worth visiting Shipley Upper, Centennial Glen and Cosmic Country.

Further up the west coast on the border between New South Wales and tropical Queensland is Mount Giraween National Park. This is a spectacular area of granite domes and boulders, although not a major climbing area. Some 70km (44 miles) south-west of Brisbane, near Boonah, is the oddly named Frogs Buttress in Mount French National Park. This is hot and humid country, more suited to snakes and lizards and the rock is

A more accessible Blue Mountains buttress at the Three Sisters.

smooth and columnar rhyolite with aretes, corners and thin cracks. The final area is the island of Tasmania, some 350km (211 miles) south of Melbourne. With its temperate maritime climate it offers an alternative to a hot and dry mainland. Much of the rock is hexagonal columns of perfect dolerite with cracks, corners and aretes.

The Organ Pipes above the capital Hobart are popular, as is Ben Lomond, Cataract Gorge and Esk Valley near Lauceston in the north. The east face of Fisherman s Cap has several long routes, but requires a two day approach and the impressive 60m (197 feet) Totem Pole is known worldwide.

Scaling the Integral Crack, Booroomba.

FACT FILE

When to Visit: Spring (September to November) and autumn (April to May). The summer (January to February) is very hot, winter (June to July) generally cold. However, April to September are good for Frog Buttress and summer is pleasant at Mount Buffalo. Tasmania is best visited in the summer (January).

Popular Climbs: With so many different areas it is almost impossible to select routes. However, the areas which no visiting rock-climber should miss are Mt Arapiles, Moonarie, the Blue Mountains and Tasmania.

Type of Climb: Cracks, walls and overhangs feature prominently. There is a variety of traditional and bolt protected routes, primarily on quartzite and sandstone, but with some granite and rhyolite.

Access: Adelaide, Melbourne, Canberra, Sydney, Brisbane and Hobart

Guidebooks: *Blue Mountains Selected Climbs, Victoria (Arapiles, Grampians and Mt Buffalo) Selected Climbs* and *Oz Rock* by Alastair Lee.

New Zealand

For European and American climbers New Zealand feels quite remote, but with the growing popularity of the Far East, Australia and Tasmania it is worth the extra effort to visit.

The North Island's highest mountain is the volcano Ruapehu. Despite rumbling on and off for the past couple of years it continues to attract many walkers in summer and skiers in winter. With its neighbours Tongariro and Ngauruhoe this area provides some fine mountain walking. To the west is the distinctive cone of Taranaki (Mt Egmont).

In comparison the South Island is a mountaineer's paradise. The Southern Alps dominate the scene and contain New Zealand's highest mountain, Mt Cook, also known by its Maori name Aorangi — Cloud Piercer. Mt Cook was finally climbed in 1894 by New Zealanders Tom Fyfe, George Graham and Jack Clarke,

shortly before the arrival of Englishman Edward Fitzgerald and Swiss guide Mattias Zurbriggen. Having missed out on Cook, the latter two made the first ascent of Mt Tasman and a number of other peaks. Zurbriggen also climbed a classic new route on Cook, soloing to the summit. Three years later he soloed the first ascent of Aconcagua, 6960m (22835 feet), the highest peak in the Americas.

The easiest approach to Cook is from Mt Cook Village, either up the Hooker Valley for the western Sheila and Caroline Faces and the south face, or up the Tasman Valley for the east and north faces. The Hooker also gives access to a range of technical ice routes on the south face of Mt Hicks. The Tasman Valley accesses the Grand Plateau and the most popular routes up Cook; the East Ridge, High Peak Route, Zurbriggen's Ridge and the Linda Glacier route. The latter is the easiest and most

Mount Dampier and the Tasman Sea at sunrise from Mount Cook Summit.

Mount Cook from the summit of Tasman: Linda Galcier in Shade.

popular route, but it is also one of the most dangerous, menaced by seracs, avalanches and crevasses in the lower section. The Grand Plateau is also the access point for the beautiful Silberhorn Arete, the most popular route on Tasman, while the technical ice climbs of the peak's Balfour Face on the south side are best approached from the Fox Glacier on the west coast.

While there are mountains north and south of the Southern Alps and all have considerable charms, only a few are worth special mention. The first is the Barrier Range to the south-west which contains Mt Aspiring, probably New Zealand's best known mountain after Mt Cook. The North-West and South-West Ridges are relatively straightforward routes on snow and ice with occasional rock. The second area is the Darren Mountains on the edge of Miford Sound to the south-west. In recent years some impressive rock routes have been put up here, but the area suffers from poor weather. Although some quality rock-climbing has been developed throughout the South Island it is not comparable to that of Thailand, Vietnam, Australia or California and for most visitors it will only provide a pleasant change to sitting out bad weather waiting to attempt the big challenges of the Southern Alps.

The summit crater of Ruapehu, North Island.

Looking up the Hooker Valley to Mt. Cook, Southern Alps.

FACT FILE

When to visit: Late November to early January for Mt Cook, and September for Mt Aspiring. The weather generally among the west coast mountains is notoriously fickle and avalanches are a serious danger in the Southern Alps. The east coast weather is generally hot and dry.

Prominent peaks: Ruapehu (2797m/9177 ft), Ngauruhoe (2290m/7513 ft), Taranaki (2518m/8261 ft), Mt Cook (3766m/12356 ft), Mt Tasman (3500m/11483 ft), Mt Hicks (3218m/10558 ft), Mt Aspiring (3027m/9931 ft).

Bases: Mt Cook Village, Fox Glacier, Wanaka, Christchurch

Activities: Mainly high quality alpine mountaineering, but lots of small crags have also been developed.

Special considerations: Good food, good wine, good huts and campsites, transport, access and health services.

Guidebooks: *The Mount Cook Guidebook* by Hugh Logan, *Mount Aspiring Region* by Graham Bishop, *Canterbury Rock* by Tim Wethey.

South America – The Andes

One of the greatest mountain chains of the world, the Andes, stretches 6,500km (4039 miles) down the western coastline of South America, from the Caribbean to Tierra del Fuego. In the north, the high volcanoes of Equador attracted interest early on, with Matterhorn conqueror Edward Whymper climbing Chimborazo, the highest, in 1880. To the south are the high mountains of Peru — the Cordilleras Blanca, Huayhuash, Vilcambamba, Urubamba and Vilcanota. Peru has some 30 peaks of 6000m (19685 feet) and above, requiring good mountaineering skills on snow, ice and rock in a frequently glacier-locked landscape. The Cordillera Blanca is the most popular region, it has superb trekking, many straightforward snow covered mountains of 5000m (16404 feet) and many long, technically difficult and committing snow and ice climbs at higher altitudes. It is also the most accessible.

Among the most popular peaks are the massive Huascaran, Alpama, the Matterhorn of the Andes and Pisco. To the south lie the slightly less accessible and less popular ranges. Among the significant peaks in the Huayhuash is Jirishanka, one of the hardest 6000m-ers in the Andes. Salkantay is the main peak in the Vilcabamba, further south towards Cuzco.

In the vicinity of Lake Titicaca, the Cordillera Apolobamba straddles the southern border between Peru and Bolivia. Peru s terrorist troubles in the mid 1980s resulted in this area and the Cordillera Real becoming more popular with mountaineers. Easily accessible from Bolivia s high mountain capital La Paz, 3700m (12139 feet), are relatively strightforward 6000m (19685 feet) peaks such as Huayna Potosi and Illimani and the beautiful but smaller Condoriri.

Huascaran Norte and Sur, highest peak in Peru, from the summit of Pisco.

South of Titicaca the Andes are shared by Bolivia, Chile and Argentina and much mountain exploring is still possible in the Cordillera Occidental and the semi-desert high mountain plateau of the Punta de Atacama. There are some 30 peaks of 6000m (19685 feet) and above, many extinct volcanoes, but the lack of water makes travel difficult. Aconcagua, the highest peak in the Americas lies wholly in Argentina. The peak was first climbed solo by the Swiss guide Matthias Zurbriggen in 1897, and the mountain is both straightforward and popular. However, this area has numerous other 6000m and 5000m (16404 feet) summits which are relatively quiet.

Almost at the tip of South America lies one of the most spectacular mountain areas of the world Patagonia. In the north lies the Patagonian Lake District, a beautiful area attracting trekkers and mountaineers. To the south and generally accessed from Argentina, the granite walls and spires surrounding FitzRoy and Cerro Torre and the equally impressive Torres del Paine in Chile, offer technical and committing climbs of the highest standard. Although the mountains are not particularly high the area is swept be fierce winds and storms and mountaineers venturing into the region need a lot of time on their hands.

Typical Andean ridge with flutings, Cordillera Blanca, Peru.

Vallunaraju, Cordillera Blanca.

Vallunaraju, Cordillera Blanca.

FACT FILE

When to visit: Equador June, July & December,
January. Peru, Bolivia June, July.
Atacama, Aconcagua, Patagonia December to March.

Prominent peaks:

Equador Chimborazo(6310m/20702 ft); Cotopaxi
(5897m/19347 ft).

Peru Huascaran Sur(6768m/22205 ft); Alpamayo
(5947m/19511 ft); Pisco (5752m/18871 ft); Jirishanka
(6094m/19993 ft); Salkantay (6271m/20574 ft).

Bolivia Illimani (6462m/21201 ft); Huayna Potosi
(6094m/19993 ft); Condoriri (5648m/18530 ft).

Argentina Aconcagua (6960m/22835 ft).

Argentina/Chile Cerro FitzRoy (3375m/11073 ft).

Chile Cerro Torre (3020m/9908 ft); Torres del Paine
(3050m/10007 ft).

Bases: Quito (Eq); Huaraz, Chiquian, Cuzco, Arequipa
(Pu); La Paz (Bo); Arica, Calama, Santiago (Ch); Salta,
Mendoza, Rio Gallegos (Ar).

Special considerations: Chile and Argentina are the
most developed, but also the most expensive. Bolivia is
cheaper and generally safe. In the past theft has been
endemic in Peru. Spanish is a distinct advantage
everywhere. There is little in the way of rescue services.

Guidebooks: *The High Andes, A Guide for Climbers* by
John Biggar, *Climbs of the Cordillera Blanca* by David
Sharman. Various guidebooks are available locally.

Activities: Mountaineering of all standards at medium
to high altitudes. Rock-climbing potential is generally
undeveloped. Patogonia offers the highest technical
difficulties on massive snow swept granite towers in
serious locations.

North America – Yosemite Valley

Situated at the northern end of the high Sierra Nevada, California, the majestic granite walls of Yosemite Valley remain the worldwide bench mark by which similar areas are judged. Today there are Arctic Yosemities, Italian Yosemities and even Crimean Yosemities, but there's only one Yosemite Valley.

The projecting nose of El Capitan rises straight from a level meadow; 900 (2953ft) metres of neck-strainingly sheer rock. Park your car, wander through the trees and in a few minutes you will be at the bottom of what is probably the biggest road-side crag in the world. Looking down the valley the rock-climber's eyes dart from cliffs built like cathedrals to towering spires until they alight on Half Dome – symbol of Yosemite National Park. Half Dome is exactly that. One side smooth and rounded, the other sliced clean off by the massive glacier which scoured through the valley tens of thousands of years ago. Climbers had beenactive in the Valley since the 1930s, but they didn't start

Half Dome in Yosemite Valley.

El Capitan, Yosemite Valley. The Nose takes a central line.

The Outer Limits, Cookie Cliff, Yosemite.

been active in the Valley since the 1930s, but they didn't start attacking and succeeding on the big walls until the late 1950s. Royal Robbins' 1957 ascent of Half Dome's vertical face was swiftly followed by Warren Harding, George Whitmore and Wayne Merry's success on El Capitan's Nose. Possibly the most aesthetic line in the Valley, the route took 45 days spread over an 18 month period. Three years later Robbins, Chuck Pratt and Tom Frost added Salathe Wall, the third of Yosemite's classic big walls.

Since then many great climbs have been added to the magnificent walls of El Capitan and Half Dome. In the main these are climbs using pitons, bolts, nuts and tape ladders for aid and assistance. While the multi-day aid climbs were being developed by 'big wallers', the 'free climbers' were putting up highly technical one and two pitch free climbs on smaller

sections of rock. During the late '70s and '80s Yosemite became a paradise for free climbers and the big walls became less fashionable.

In the past decade things have developed further. Today aid climbing is back in fashion, not just the simple hammering in of pegs and bolts, but also the cunning use of devices which can be placed and then removed without damaging the rock. Instead of long lines of bolts, today's big walls can involve long sections without protection where progress is only possible via small metal hooks kept in place on tiny ruggosities in the rock through body weight. The free climbers haven't been dormant either, but have turned their attentions from smaller technical routes on the lower crags to free-climbing the big walls, starting with Paul Piana and Todd Skinner's 1988 free ascent of Salathe Wall. The route which caught the public imagination, however, was Lynn Hill's 1993 free ascent of The Nose. The following year Hill went one better, free climbing every pitch in a single day. Free climbing continues on the big walls with Alex and Thomas Huber's stunning ascent of El Nino on El Cap's North America Wall in 1998.

Descent from El Capitan, Yosemite Valley.

Steep face climbing on the granite domes of Tuolumne Meadows, Yosemite National Park.

The renaissance in big wall climbing in Yosemite means that classic routes like the Nose and Salathe are more popular than ever, although most teams continue to use lots of aid and climb the routes over a number of days.

FACT FILE

When to Visit: April and May, September and October
Peaks and Routes: Big walls and multi-pitch – Salathe, The Nose, Zodiac on El Capitan; South Face, The Prow, Astro Man on Washington Column; Regular Northwest Face, Direct Northwest Face, Snake Dike on Half Dome. Shorter free rock routes – Cookie Cliff, Central Pillar of Frenzy on Middle Cathedral Rock.

Type of Climb: Free and aided multi-day and multi-pitch big walls. Multi and single pitch traditional free climbs, mostly crack and face. Multi-pitch generally bolt protected friction slabs.

Guidebooks: *Yosemite Climbs, Big Walls* by Don Reid; Yosemite Climbs, Free Climbs.

Access: Highway 140 from Merced. The Valley has a loop road, mostly one way.

Parking: Possible at most points of access to the main cliffs.

Eldorado Canyon

With good reason, Eldorado Canyon is probably the most famous of the climbing areas in the Boulder/Denver area. Its soaring walls – up to 700 feet of gorgeous golden, orange, red, and brown Fountain Formation sandstone will elevate the spirit of any visitor. Raptors circle high above in updrafts. South Boulder Creek's waters carve through the canyon's bottom. Eldorado has attracted climbers, hikers, and picnick-ers alike for years. It has an almost mystical appeal, especially for climbers.

Climbing is possible most days due to 300 days of sunshine a year and Colorado's generally mild and dry clime. However, at times, weather can be extreme and/or change rapidly. April through October is the prime time with spring and fall being best. Summertime heat can be escaped on shaded faces and wintertime cool can be enjoyed on sunbathed faces.

Below: Climbing Yellow Edge, Eldorado Canyon.

Eldorado Canyon, Colorado.

Eldorado Canyon lies 6 miles south of Boulder at the west end of State Highway 170. Most crags mentioned lie within and are accessed through the state park. Park regulations include day use only and access fees. There are limited but strict (Feb 1–July 31) cliff closures for nesting raptors. To place new fixed hardware (pins, bolts, etc.), you must apply and get approval. Most approaches vary from two to 30 minutes. Access to Mickey Mouse Wall, above and a mile to the south of Eldorado, is currently in question due to land issues. In recent years, raptor protection has closed the crag Feb 1–July 31. Approach time is 1 hour.

Parking spaces are limited and sometimes are unavailable on busy summer weekends. The two primary areas are at the east and west ends of the public access road. Park at the west end for access to the Rincon, Shirt Tail Peak, upper West Ridge, and Peanuts walls. Beware, parking in Eldorado Springs often results in parking fines.

Most of the 1000-plus climbs in the Eldorado Canyon area involve a variety of face, crack, and slab techniques and often reward grace over brute force. Cruxes are often brief but

Scaling the Genesis crag, Eldorado Canyon.

Climbing the Redgarden Wall, Eldorado Canyon.

thought-provoking. Climbs are often done for the joy of the experience rather than the grade of difficulty. The rock quality is, in general, quite good, although there are weaker layers. Beautiful colours of rock and lichen stimulate your eyes. Cracks here are often discontinuous. The rock is typically off-vertical to vertical with infrequent overhangs. It helps to be able to recognize poison ivy. Few true sport climbs exist here. As a result, Eldorado lacks cutting edge sport climbing but rather emphasizes lower to mid-range climbing.

There are many crags within a small area here. The main crags (clockwise starting on your left looking west) are: Bastille, Lower & Upper Peanuts, Mickey Mouse (high and over a ridge), Rincon, Shirt Tail Peak, West Ridge, Redgarden (the largest), Whale's Tail, and Wind Tower. The Redgarden Wall boasts the longest and most routes.

Climbs here are predominantly naturally protected. Numerous climbs require two 50m ropes to descend, although few routes require double rope technique. Fixed pins and old 1/4" bolts are always suspect. Chipping is simply not tolerated. Avoid littering.

FACT FILE

When to visit: Best April to October, although year-round climbing is possible.

Type of Climb: Mostly traditional face and crack climbing on solid sandstone.

Highest Peak: Shirt Tail Peak, 7542 ft.

Access: Highway 170, through Eldorado Canyon State Park.

Parking: In Eldorado Canyon State Park. Can be limited.

Canada – British Columbia

British Columbia stretches the full length of the Canadian Rocky Mountains from the Yukon to the US border and contains so much quality rock that a brief overview of the best areas will have to suffice.

For rock-climbers, the primary destination will probably be the massive granite faces above the town of Squamish, some 65 kilometres north of Vancouver. The area has been popular with climbers since the early 1960s and offers many excellent and technical routes, both on the 500m (1640 ft) face of Squamish Chief and on smaller more recently developed cliffs. The rock is high quality, fine grained microgranite with all types

of routes and both traditional and bolt protection. Some 800 kilometres (497 miles) north of Vancouver at the southern tip of the Coast Range is Mt Waddington. With its long snowy ridge of granite pinnacles, it is one of the most impressive mountains in North America. However, despite this, relative ease of access and an abundance of big granite walls in the vicinity, the area is not popular.

Waddington's South Face, nominated as one of America's Fifty Classic Climbs in the book of the same name, has only had seven ascents since the book's publication in the 1970s! This is certainly an area to escape the crowds. Waddington was not put

Tackling The Apron, Squamish.

on the map until 1922 and only named in the 1930s. Its first ascent was in 1936 by Fritz Wiessner and Bill House.

Further east, the mountains of the Selkirk range have attracted mountaineers since the 1880s. Precipitation here is high, like in the Coast Range, and the area is heavily glaciated, giving a complex mountain terrain. However, it is the peaks of the Bugaboos in the Purcell Range to the east and south that capture the imagination of most climbers. These glacier-surrounded granite towers are not high in altitude, but very impressive in stature. The celebrated Austrian mountaineer Conrad Kain helped open up the area, climbing the South Ridge of Bugaboo Spire in 1916. Since then many superb and technical routes have been added to their granite walls. East again

A steep ascent up The Main Event at Squamish.

Ascending Crescent Crack, the Malamute, Squamish.

Overly hanging – out on the Malamute, Squamish.

lie the impressive peaks of Rocky Mountains on The Great Divide between BC and Alberta. Peaks like Mt Robson and Mt Assiniboine offer both traditional and technical mountaineering challenges.

Much of the northern reaches of British Columbia are hard to access although good climbing and mountaineering certainly exists. One area which has seen development over the years is around Stikine in the northern part of the Coast Range on the border between BC and the south-east leg of Alaska. Here various granite towers and faces have been climbed in the vicinity of the Devil's Thumb. Note that the weather is often unsettled.

FACT FILE

When to visit: British Columbia has a very maritime climate, with much precipitation. Squamish – July and August. For the mountain areas summer is best for all areas, unless attempting the big snow and ice faces of the Rockies, in which case spring or autumn.

Peaks and Routes: Squamish Chief Apron, Grand Wall – Diedre, Banana Peel, Mercy Me, University Wall, Apron Strings; Mt Waddington (4042m/13,261 ft); South-East Chimneys; Bugaboos – North Tower (3399m/11,152 ft), South Tower (3307m/10,850 ft), Bugaboo Spire (3176m/10,420 ft), Snowpatch Spire (3063m/10,049 ft); Rockies – Mt Robson (3954m/12,972 ft); Mt Assiniboine (3618m/11,870 ft).

Type of Climb: Squamish offers cracks and slabs of fine granite. Mt Waddington offers alpine mountaineering on granite peaks in remote locations, the Bugaboos are mountain rock climbs and walls and the Rockies classic alpine mountaineering on ridges and faces.

Access: Squamish is easily accessed from Highway 99 north of Vancouver. Mt Waddington is best approached by car to Tatla Lake and light aircraft to the Tiedemann Glacier. The Bugaboos are approached from the town of Parson off Highway 93.

Guidebooks: *Squamish Rockclimber's Guide* by Kevin McLane, *Bugaboos* by Kevin McLane, *Mount Waddington Range* by Don Serl.

Greenland

One of the biggest islands in the world, the core of Greenland is a massive ice cap rising to about 3000m (9843 feet) above sea level. Over the years considerable mountaineering and rock-climbing has taken place in summer when the coastal fjords become free from pack-ice. Transportation costs can be high and the weather mixed and consequently, Greenland is an area which goes in and out of fashion.

One of the most fashionable areas at present are the big walls east of the Tasermiut fjord, north of Nanortalik on Greenland's southern tip. This area is similar in many ways to northern Norway where heavy glaciation has left some impressive granite faces, particularly those of Ulamertossuaq and Nulamertossuaq, towering some 800m (2625 feet) above the fjord. Over the years a number of routes now exist on the faces and there is considerable scope for development throughout the area.

The most popular area of Greenland are the Staunings Alps in Scoresby Land immediately north-west of Iceland. This area offers a range of climbing, both long rock routes and alpine style mountaineering. Many other coastal ranges have been visited including the Lemon Mountains in the Denmark Strait, south of Scoresby Land near Kangerlussuaq.

View downto Tasermuit fjord, SW Greenland.

Granite Peaks above Tasermuit fjord.

FACT FILE

When to Visit: June, July.

Popular climbs: Moby Dick, a 1300m (4265 ft), multi-day big wall on Ulamertossuaq has had two ascents, but most climbers come to Greenland for exploration, climbing new peaks and new routes, rather than repeating existing climbs.

Type of Climb: The Tasermiut fjord walls are mainly granite, the Lemon Mountains gneiss. Rock-climbing, multi-pitch rock routes and alpine mountaineering are all possible.

Access: Greenland can only be accessed via Denmark and Iceland. Travel within Greenland is by small plane and boat.

Self Rescue

Self-rescue in this context refers to the ability of a climber to rescue his/her partner in the event of a fall, when for one reason or another, the partner cannot help him/herself. This situation may arise because the fallen climber has become unconscious or perhaps more commonly because they are dangling free from the rock on the end of the rope and cannot regain the point where they fell. In either situation the belayer will be tied into the belay and holding the dead rope. The live rope will be loaded with the weight of the fallen climber. Somehow the belayer must rescue the climber. If the climber appears to be unconscious it is also important to do this fairly quickly as asphyxiation can result from hanging motionless in a harness.

You should not attempt or practise any of these techniques without the guidance of a mountaineering instructor. It is however useful to understand the principles of self rescue and the techniques that are available. You should always carry two prusik loops clipped somewhere to your harness and a small pen-knife for use in these situations.

If a fall occurs, and your partner appears unable to help him/herself, it will be your responsibility to extract them from the situation. Before doing anything, think carefully through your options. Is it possible to simply lower the climber to the ground or to a ledge? Are there other climbers nearby who could help

Sling tied in a Klemheist knot.

in the rescue? Consider all the alternatives and take the simplest and most effective course of action, rather than embarking immediately on an elaborate rescue plan.

If you cannot lower the climber to the ground or back to the belay by simply letting out rope and you have considered all your other alternatives, it will be necessary for you the belayer to enact the rescue. This means that you must escape the system of loaded ropes into which you are tied. To do this you

Tied off Belay device above stich plate.

Escaping the system.

Example of a Prusik Knot tied on a double rope.

will need to transfer the weight from the loaded live rope to the anchors. First, tie off the belay device using a half hitch round the back bar of the belay krab or around the rope. This knot can be released again under load. This will free your hands to clip a sling into the anchors you can reach and make a new independent central point anchor. Tie a prusik loop onto the live rope and attach it to the new anchor point you have made, using slings or extenders. Back this up by tying the dead rope into another anchor krab using a tied off Italian hitch. You can then release the tied off belay device and let out a little rope until the weight is taken on the prusik loop. This will allow you to unclip the belay device and free yourself from the system. The dead rope is then pulled up tight using the Italian hitch and tied off again with half hitches. Pulling the hitch up tight should allow you to recover the prusik loop from the loaded rope, with the weight now being borne by the Italian hitch.

If the climber is unconscious, it is imperative to get to him/her quickly to prevent asphyxiation. You will need to do this by ascending or descending the tight rope using your remaining prusik loop(s) and if necessary a sling in a klemheist knot. One prusik will be attached to a leg loop for you to stand up in and this can also be clipped to your harness loosely as a backup. The other loop will be attached directly to the harness and used to

hang on while the leg loop is moved upwards. Alternately remove and re-attach each loop to get past these runners, which cannot be unclipped. On reaching the casualty, attach a Parisian baudrier and clip this to a prusik loop or klemheist knot on the load rope to support the unconscious climber, and carry out any necessary basic first aid.

On a traverse pitch scenario, straight hoisting or lowering will obviously be of no use on a multi-pitch crag or on many sea cliff routes. In this situation it will be necessary to move out along the rope as described above, bringing the other end of the rope with you. Attach this end to the fallen climber before returning to the belay stance. This rope can then be hoisted in as the other is let out. In this way the climber can be brought back to the belay from a fall off a traverse.

If the climber has become unable to move below the belay while seconding a pitch, and lowering to the ground isn t an option, it will be necessary to hoist him or her up to the belay stance. If they are unconscious you will need to escape the system and descend the rope to affix a Parisian baudrier and remove the runners which would otherwise prevent a straight hoist.

Once back on the belay there are a variety of hoisting techniques which could be employed, although the most popular are probably the hip hoist and the Z pulley hoist.

To hip hoist, first escape the system as before, tying off the dead rope with an Italian hitch to a high anchor point. Transfer the weight onto this hitch and remove the prusik loop from the anchor. Clip this prusik instead to the belay loop on the harness. Hold the dead rope from the Italian hitch in one hand, and crouch down and push the prusik down the live rope with the other. As you stand up with a powerful push of your legs, the prusik will lock and lift the climber upwards. At the same time pull as much rope as you can though the Italian hitch. Hold the weight once more on the Italian hitch and reposition the prusik down the live rope and repeat the process until the climber is on the belay.

The Z pulley hoist is perhaps the most effective. To do this, escape the system as before, but rather than tie an Italian hitch on a high anchor, instead affix a small prusik loop at this anchor and run the rope through the krab. Make sure you have tied off the dead rope to another anchor krab to back up the prusik. Attach another prusik loop as far down the live rope as you can reach and clip a krab into it. Clip the dead rope through this krab and you will have made a simple Z pulley. As you pull on the dead rope the lower prusik should lock and lift the weight of the climber. Rope will run through the upper anchor krab and the prusik loop attached to it. When you have taken in the rope as far as you can, the upper prusik should lock, taking the weight allowing you to reposition the lower prusik back down the loaded rope. If the climber is conscious, perhaps hanging free and unable to ascend the rope, the Z pulley can be simplified considerably by lowering the pulley krab to the climber which he/she attaches to the belay loop on their harness. This means that only one prusik is required for security, to lock-off the top anchor krab, and avoids the need for continually repositioning the lower pulley point.

Once you have managed to bring the injured climber back to the belay it is necessary to recover the ropes and begin the abseil descent to the ground. This will be significantly easier if you have been climbing on double ropes, because you can tie them together with a double fisherman s knot though an anchor and abseil 50 metres (164 feet) at a time. You will still be able to recover the ropes by pulling them through the anchor. With a single 50 metre (164 foot) rope it is possible to abseil only 25 metres (82 feet) while still being able to recover the rope. You can then release the tied-off belay device and let out a little rope until the weight is taken on the prusik loop.

To abseil with an unconscious or injured climber, use a short sling. Tie an overhand knot in the middle, clip one end to your belay loop, and the other to your partner s belay loop. Clip the belay device through both loops in the middle of the sling, across the overhand knot. Then attach the device to the ropes as usual. You should also use a French prusik attached to the dead rope, which is clipped to the leg loop of your harness. This will lock off the abseil device should you let go of the dead rope inadvertently. Only use a short French prusik as a dead man s hand on the leg loop wnen the belay device is extended away from the belay loop on the harness. This will prevent the prusik knot releasing.

Extreme care should be taken when abseiling with an unconscious climber.

First Aid

This section cannot hope to cover everything a competent first aider should know. Here we have only covered the most essential information necessary to preserve life. In particular we have not covered the treatment of bleeding, fractures and burns, which are all fairly common injuries in the outdoors. We have however included a description of hypothermia and its treatment, and a section on altitude related problems for those destined for the higher summits of the world.

It is useful to consider the sequence of actions which should be taken should you be at the scene of an accident in the outdoors. Firstly, you should ensure both your own safety and the safety of the casualty. Prevention of further accidents must be the first thing on your mind. Therefore, take a deep breath and assess the situation carefully before you rush in.

First aid is always applied using the simple ABC rule. This stands for Airway, Breathing and Circulation. These are the most critical factors to address and in that order. Therefore, firstly

It is important to monitor the casualty's vital signs.

make sure that there is a clear air passage to the lungs. If necessary use a finger to clear the airway of blood or vomit. Having made sure of a clear airway, ensure that the casualty is breathing. Then check the circulation to ascertain the presence and strength of the heart beat.

First aid is all about stabilising the situation so that the unfortunate casualty survives as comfortably as possible until help arrives. This means you need to ensure that the casualty remains stable and that help does indeed arrive. If you are alone this presents obvious problems and there will be difficult choices to make. The rule of thumb is to never leave a casualty alone if you can possibly avoid it. Therefore, if possible send other competent people for help. Make sure these people know where they are going and send with them the following information, in writing if possible.

The exact location of the accident. Provide a six figure grid reference if at all possible, or the name of the route you are on. The number of casualties involved at the scene. A brief description of what has happened, i.e. fall, avalanche, stone fall etc. The nature and severity of the injuries and suspected injuries. Any treatments applied so far. The first aid competence level of those remaining with the casualty. Any other information which will be of help to those effecting the rescue. As in your climbing experiences, maintaining a calm mind and making sensible decisions is as important as the first aid you carry out. Make as certain as you can that those who go for help have the right information before they leave, and that they are not likely to get lost on the way out.

You should continually monitor the casualty s vital signs to check their well being. The vital signs are breathing, breathing rate, pulse, pulse rate, regularity and strength. Checking these variables every three to five minutes and recording it will be useful to the medical services later. You should also check the level of consciousness of the casualty.

If you are in the situation of caring for an unconscious casualty your primary concerns should be ABC. If the casualty is lying on their back you should tilt the head slightly back by placing one hand on the forehead and two fingers of the other hand under the chin. A gentle push on the chin will tilt the head back and open the throat, making breathing easier. You must continually

Place casualty in the recovery position only if it is safe to do so, and spine and neck injuries are not suspected.

monitor the breathing of an unconscious casualty because vomiting is very common as consciousness is regained, and this could easily block the airway. Another common cause of death of the unconscious casualty is the tongue blocking the airway.

Measure and record the level of consciousness of the casualty along the following AVPU scale.

- ● **Alert – Responds spontaneously and coherently.**
- ● **Vocal – Responds to vocal stimulus.**
- ● **Pain – Responds to pain such as pinching.**
- ● **Unresponsive – Responds to no forms of stimulation.**

If possible place the casualty into the recovery position, on one side with the face slightly down so that airway blockage is less likely.

HYPOTHERMIA

The effects of cold and wind chill on the human body and mind must be understood so that they can be recognised quickly, both in oneself and others. Hypothermia affects not only the body but in its more advanced stages the mind as well. When this happens, our ability to make sound judgements is severely impaired and the seriousness of the situation rises exponentially. For this reason it is necessary to be able to recognise all of the stages of hypothermia, from its early beginnings as a cold nose through to the behavioural changes of more advanced stages.

The first signs to look for are ordinary enough. Numb hands and feet and vigorous shivering are fairly common in the mountain environment at the best of times. What you must make sure of is that these symptoms are not allowed to persist, or get

If you do get frostbite, keep the area frozen until you get to a hospital.

significantly worse. As long as remedial action is taken in time the danger will be avoided. Often this means simply adjusting your clothing, not being lazy about zips, hoods or gloves, or perhaps moving on rather than taking a long rest. In climbing situations you may be tied to the mountainside for hours at a time, belaying your climbing partner who seems to be taking forever to climb the next pitch. In this instance it is especially important to avoid getting too cold as you cannot simply get up and walk about to warm up. Make sure your clothing is keeping out as much cold as it can. This may sound obvious, however sometimes it takes a good deal of patience and perseverance simply to adjust a fiddly zip with numb hands and gloves on. Breathing down the inside of the jacket is another technique used to keep warm air inside the coat. When things get worse still you can always try jumping up and down or running on the spot.

The more serious symptoms of hypothermia to watch out for are:
- **Irrational and/or unreasonable behaviour**
- **Lethargy and apathy**
- **Argumentative or even violent behaviour**
- **Unwillingness to accept or appreciate that something is wrong**
- **Slurring of the speech and blurring of vision (only in some instances)**

Clearly the majority of these symptoms are likely to make the situation very much worse. For example lethargy and apathy can lead people to be careless with their clothing or their situation.

It is therefore vital to make sure that such a negative spiral of events does not occur in the first place.

In cases of mild hypothermia get the casualty out of the cold environment (into a tent, snow hole or emergency bivouac bag), and replace wet clothing with dry. Food and warm drinks may be given to the casualty. In severe cases of hypothermia protection from the weather and insulation from further heat loss are very important. However, re-warming should not be attempted in very severe cases. Give nothing to eat or drink and move as little as possible. Even in the absence of a pulse you should never attempt CPR (cardio-pulmonary resuscitation) on a victim of extreme hypothermia.

ALTITUDE PROBLEMS

If you are going to be climbing, or even trekking, in some of the higher areas of the world you should understand altitude related health problems such as acute mountain sickness, pulmonary oedema and cerebral oedema. Such problems are thought to occur because of the rapid fall in air pressure as height is gained. Such changes in exterior air pressure mean that the body must adjust its internal pressure balance. This is achieved by the body losing water as altitude is gained, and problems occur generally when this adjustment cannot be made rapidly enough, causing water imbalance in the body, the lungs or the brain.

The best advice is to gain altitude slowly in order to give the body time to acclimatise to new altitudes. Drink plenty of water and make sure that you continue to urinate as normal. Remaining

A bivouac bag is the most important piece of survival equipment. Everyone should carry one in winter.

Superlative flying from the Chamonix rescue services, looking for climbers missing in the range.

relaxed in your environment may also help the body to function normally in terms of its ability to balance the water pressures across its membranes. Go high during the day time and sleep low at night to help the acclimatisation process.

Most importantly, listen to the signals your body sends out and act accordingly. If you feel bad or have a headache, descend. Do not ignore such symptoms, as it is much better to acclimatise slowly than try to force the issue. You should certainly be aware of the deadly nature of altitude related problems. Once

pulmonary oedema or cerebral oedema set in the situation is very serious indeed, so it is much better to descend earlier rather than later.

Index

Credits & Acknowledgements

Contributed Text:

Gary Latter

George McEwan

Leo Paik

Tom Prentice

Rob Savoye

Picture Credits
(t = top, b = bottom, l = left, r = right)

Andy Clarke
13, 54, 59, 60, 63, 64, 74, 75, 76, 77, 78, 79, 80b,
84, 85b, 88, 89, 90, 101, 102t, 104, 105t

Michael Gray
1, 6b, 7, 8, 12b, 21, 23, 24, 25, 33, 34, 35, 36, 37,
38t, 40, 41, 43, 45, 46, 48, 49t, 50, 51,
52, 53, 56, 57, 61, 66, 67, 68, 69, 70, 72, 73, 95,
96, 97

Gary Latter
9, 10, 18, 29, 38b, 39, 42, 55, 80t, 85t, 86, 87t,
91l, 92, 108r, 109r, 110, 111, 112, 113, 114, 115

Robin McAllister
12t, 17, 30, 65b, 71

Tom Prentice
14, 44, 47, 58, 81, 82, 83, 87b, 91r, 93, 94, 102b,
103, 105b, 106, 107, 108l, 109l, 121b, 123

Duncan Robertson
19, 20, 22, 26, 27

Shout Picture Library
117, 118, 119, 120, 121t, 122

Chris Townsend
116

Bill Wright
98l, 99, 100

Others
Sarah Campbell 11b, Graeme Leggett 65t, Dave
McGimpsey 11t, Karen Martin 6t, S. Mearns 49b,
Sarah Harris 98.

The author and publisher would also like to thank the following for
supplying much of the equipment used in photography:

Paramo Ltd

Sprayway Ltd

HB Climbing Equipment

Glasgow Climbing Centre